Coins from the Soil
A Guide to the Buried Coinage of Britain

Coins from the Soil
A Guide to the Buried Coinage of Britain

by
Michael Cuddeford

Mount Publications
2008

© Mount Publications,
PO Box 1916,
CHELMSFORD,
CM3 1EY.

ISBN 978-1-900571-11-1

CONTENTS

FOREWORD
by Dr. Roger Bland O.B.E., Head of the Department of Portable Antiquities and Treasure at the British Museum

Amongst the most common finds made by metal-detector users in Britain are coins, medals and tokens and over 110,000 are now recorded on the Portable Antiquities Scheme (PAS) database. And yet identifying them can present many challenges to the uninitiated and Mike Cuddeford's book fills an important gap in presenting a short and accessible guide to the main varieties of coins and tokens found in Britain.

Because the coins of some periods, such as the late Roman Empire, are such common finds, often surviving in poor condition, they can easily end up in detector-users' 'junk boxes' without any record of where they were found. Mike Cuddeford rightly stresses how much information can be obtained even from these little-regarded Roman 'grots' if they are properly recorded. The systematic study of such objects can add so much to our understanding of how people used – and lost - coins in the past. This book also contains a fascinating account of an experiment carried out by the author on how hoards of coins can become dispersed in the ploughsoil.

Numismatists were the amongst first scholars to recognise the importance of recording coins found by detector-users and projects like the Celtic Coin Index (now incorporated into the PAS database), the Fitzwilliam Museum's Early Medieval Corpus and the PAS database demonstrate how much knowledge can be obtained from the systematic recording of coin finds.

If this book encourages more people to keep records of all their finds, including the 'grots', it will have fulfilled its purpose.

PREFACE AND ACKNOWLEDGEMENTS

The title of this book will no doubt surprise some people, who would not imagine that there was any significant body of coins to be found buried in the ground, apart from the occasional hoard which makes the headlines. It will be no surprise however to archaeologists and metal detector users, who routinely unearth individual coins in surprising numbers, as well as professional numismatists and collectors who examine and acquire them.

Coins have been used in Britain since the late Iron Age, and ever since they were used they have been lost, discarded or deliberately buried, and in consequence are often found again by later generations. Unlike other artefacts, coins are usually closely dateable, and this gives them a particular archaeological value, although caution is needed in determining when they may actually have been lost. Coins are also sometimes the only prolific type of artefact from a particular period, and the accurate plotting and recording of coin finds can be of immense value in building up a wider picture of the history of an area. It is the purpose of this book to provide a guide to the identification of the more commonly found coins, to present an overview of coin use and loss in Britain against their historical background, and to examine possible processes of how they were used and lost. The mechanisms by which coins may come to be buried in the first place, and how they can be dispersed by agricultural activity, may not always be as straightforward as might be supposed, and anyone involved with the recovery of coins, whether single finds or a scattered hoard, needs to be aware of all the possible variables. There is inevitably going to be some geographical bias with regard to the coins listed, as many of the data derive from metal detecting, which is predominantly carried out on arable land in the more populous areas of Britain. However, based on the information now currently available, it is reasonable to submit that the coins listed herein represent an accurate overview of coin use and loss in Britain over the last two thousand years.

Deciding what to include, and what to exclude in a book of this nature is not straightforward. It is certainly not intended to be an exhaustive catalogue, as such catalogues already exist and some coins, particularly those of high denomination, rarely if ever occur as individual losses. For this reason only representative examples of certain coin types are included, but from these it should be possible to narrow down any find sufficiently to enable the appropriate catalogue to be consulted - a bibliography is provided at the end of this book. A number of foreign coins that occur as British site finds, some common, some less so, have also been included, as these fall outside of the main catalogues familiar to British coin finders. The coins that are included here are a sample reflecting the types and denominations excavated and recorded over the past thirty years or so. This is based on personal experience, archaeological reports, numismatic journals and the Portable Antiquities Scheme database. The geographical area examined is confined to the mainland of Britain alone, and excludes Northern Ireland, the Isle of Man and the Channel Isles as their numismatic heritage is quite different, and instances of coin finds considerably less frequent.

The book is divided into chapters based on conventional historical periods. A separate chapter includes 'early post-medieval' coins, as a way of dealing with a period of considerable numismatic and historical diversity. This broadly covers a period from the latter part of the fifteenth century until around the middle of the seventeenth century. There is inevitably some degree of overlap when classifying certain issues that span more than one period. The most significant numismatic event during this time was the general adoption of the screw press as a means of manufacturing coins. Until the late fifteenth century coins were normally produced manually by striking the coin dies together with a hammer, and coins struck by this method are referred to as 'hammered coins'. These have a distinctive and often irregular appearance. This method of production was gradually supplanted following the introduction of hand operated screw presses, which in Britain did not become the sole method of coining until the latter part of the seventeenth century. The serrations around the edges of modern coins are sometimes also referred to as milling, but are more correctly known as 'graining'. The blank of the coin itself is referred to as the 'flan'.

Acknowledgements: I am most grateful to the following who kindly allowed me access to their catalogues, archives or collections for the purpose of illustration: The Classical Numismatic Group (CNG), Chris Rudd, Mike Vosper, A.H. Baldwin & Sons, Spink & Son, Paul & Bente Withers (Galata), Tony Holmes, Bob Thomas, Keith Cullum, Alastair Wardle, Roger Barrett, David Powell, Andrew Palmer, Alfred Daines and Frank Knights. I am also indebted to Roger Bland for kindly writing the foreword, and to Jim Patterson for enquiries made regarding coin finds from within the metal detecting fraternity.

1
IRON AGE COINS

Historical Background

Amongst the peoples of Iron Age Europe were some known by the Ancient Greeks as 'Keltoi'; these were evidently a culturally discrete group, although no doubt as diverse in many ways as the nations of modern Europe still are. The Romans recognised three main groupings, corresponding roughly to modern Germany, France and Spain. Within France, then known as Gallia, Julius Caesar sub-divided the population as the Aquitani, Belgae and Celtae, from whence comes the modern name 'Celtic'. This is now used as a general term to describe the non-classical peoples of Iron Age western Europe, and in particular their distinctive artistic tradition and coins.

The peoples of Britain who first began using coins were of common stock with their European neighbours, and ethnically may well have been the same people who built Stonehenge. Archaeologists have long debated as to what extent new cultural developments were the result of invasion, or simply the migration of ideas and technology, but it is clear that by the late Iron Age there were close social and political links between the populations of south-eastern Britain and north-western France.

Caesar was the first classical writer to deal at any length with the peoples of Britain, and during the course of his campaigns in Gaul he undertook two separate invasions of the island. Whilst his accounts must be taken with a degree of caution, as he was writing for political effect, we have for the first time an idea of some of the population, and the names of some of their leaders. By linking this sparse documentary evidence to the archaeological evidence, and in particular the coinage, we can begin to build up a picture of late Iron Age Britain.

Iron Age coins are conventionally classified according to tribal groupings, and this can provide a means of initial identification, as many groupings are of quite distinctive style. Although the British tribal areas are based on historical records dating from Roman times, there is no way of knowing if the names that we give to the tribes were necessarily correct at the time the coins were struck. Some tribes may have been subsumed by others, or their boundaries changed. Thus there are various sub-groups of coins that might relate to absorbed tribes, the names of which are now unknown. In his account of his invasions of Britain, Caesar lists a number of tribes that cannot now be located geographically, and also mentions the names of various kings who cannot be identified with any known coins. Because of this, it is now more usual to attribute coins to the geographical areas in which they are generally found, rather than use possibly incorrect tribal names. The following concordance indicates the geographical locations of the traditional tribal names as used in the past:

North-Eastern. *Corieltauvi* (formerly known as the *Coritani*): Lincolnshire, Leicestershire, Nottinghamshire, Humberside and perhaps parts of South Yorkshire.

Eastern. *Iceni*: Norfolk, north Cambridgeshire and north Suffolk.

North Thames. *Trinovantes*: Essex, south Cambridgeshire and south Suffolk. *Catuvellauni*: Hertfordshire, but expanded to take in the *Trinovantes'* territory as well as much of the East Midlands and Home Counties.

South-Eastern. *Cantii*: Kent.

Southern. *Atrebates*: Berkshire, Surrey, Sussex and parts of Hampshire. *Regni*: Hampshire.

South-Western. *Durotriges*: Dorset and parts of Hampshire, Somerset and Wiltshire.

Western. *Dobunni*: Gloucestershire, and parts of Hereford and Worcester, Somerset, Oxfordshire and Wiltshire.

The Coinage

Prior to the introduction of coins, it is possible that certain other objects had a currency value. It was once thought that Bronze Age penannular gold rings may have been used in this way, although there is no evidence for it, but we are told by Caesar that some British tribes used iron bars as well as coins and blade-shaped iron ingots have certainly been excavated in hoard-like contexts. The Romans, themselves an Iron Age tribe, used bronze ingots by weight, and it is possible that some Bronze Age metalwork finds from Britain represent either contemporary or later use in a currency context. It is perhaps unlikely that any of these objects were used in a conventional purchasing capacity, but rather represent stored wealth.

The earliest actual coins found in Britain that are likely to have been contemporary losses are a small number of Greek bronzes struck at Carthage in the third century BC, which have been discovered on a few late Iron Age sites in the south-east. Perhaps brought back by warriors who had fought abroad as mercenaries, or imported through trade, it is unclear whether they actually had a monetary use.

Bronze coin of Carthage, found in Kent

The peoples of late Iron Age western Europe began striking coins based on Greek prototypes in the third century BC. By the middle of the second century BC imported Gaulish coins were being used in Britain, and by the end of the century coins were being manufactured here. Iron Age coins are often very distinctive, copied from classical prototypes but sometimes with amazing abstraction.

Phillip II Greek stater, c.359-336 BC. This was the prototype for all early Iron Age uninscribed gold staters that are found in Britain. The obverse head of Apollo and the reverse charioteer evolved into the abstract elements that can be found in subsequent Iron Age issues.

In the years leading up to the Roman invasion of AD 43, some British coins became very Romanised in style and borrowed heavily from Roman iconography. The earliest British coins were uninscribed, but from about the middle of the first century BC and following the tradition of their Gaulish counterparts, British rulers began putting their names, and in some cases mint town names, on their coins. Most are abbreviations, and the full names and identities of many to whom the legends refer are unknown.

Iron Age coinage in Britain was not generally based on the tri-metallic system of the Romans. Many tribes only used gold and silver, and even where bronze was used, there is not an even statistical distribution of denominations. It is quite possible that Iron Age coins were used not only as a means of commercial exchange, but also for religious and other social functions.

A major characteristic of most Iron Age coins is the profile of the flan, or blank upon which the design is struck. This typically tends to be dished, or 'scyphate', and even when totally illegible this characteristic can often be sufficient to attribute a coin to the period. In some regions, particularly the Thames Valley area, many bronzes may be found and it is important to be able to distinguish illegible British coins from Roman ones, as it can have considerable statistical implications in evaluating activity on any given site. Shown here is a typical cross section of an Iron Age coin compared to a Roman one.

(a) Iron Age coin profile (b) Roman coin profile

Another clue, although not without exception, is that early British base metal coins, due to the alloy used, tend to have a more coppery colour as opposed to the brassier look of most Roman coins of similar size. Thus even with an illegible specimen, a combination of flan profile together with metal appearance can often provide enough clues to attribute a coin to the correct period.

The peoples of Iron Age Europe were highly accomplished metallurgists, and the weights of their coins, particularly gold and silver, tend to fall within quite close parameters. In the Middle Ages, wheat grains were used as the basis for a weighing system, as they are remarkably uniform in weight. It is quite possible that a similar system was employed in the Iron Age. Ceramic moulds presumed to be for the making of coin blanks are known, and if metal was added through the medium of filings, very accurate weights could be obtained. Such a method would also have readily facilitated alloying, which had been perfected to a fine art, with some gold coins containing large quantities of copper and silver and yet still retaining a gold appearance. In addition to alloying gold, gold and silver plating was practised, and if the plating is intact such coins can be very hard to tell from solid examples, as the weights can be very similar. Such coins may have been the work of forgers, or even perhaps official issues struck at times of gold shortage, or maybe for votive purposes. Most Iron Age coins were die-struck with two exceptions. An early series of coins produced in both Gaul and southern Britain were cast in strips using a copper-alloy with a high tin content. This distinctive alloy is sometimes referred to 'potin'. Another group comprises cast bronze 'staters' produced in south-west Britain.

We have no knowledge of the names that may have been used to describe the various denominations. Iron Age gold coins are referred to as 'staters', after the Greek prototype of that name, and fractions thereof. Other coins in silver and copper-alloy are simply referred to as 'units', although some of the silver coins approximate to the Roman *'quinarius'*.

Site Finds

Unlike any subsequent coinage, Iron Age gold coins occur with regularity, although they are still relatively speaking very rare. Staters and their fractions turn up across the whole of the coin-using zone of Britain. In some areas that did not have a copper-alloy coinage, silver units can occur with frequency, such as in the North East and Eastern regions. They are however much scarcer further south and may even be outnumbered by gold. Some may only have been struck for votive purposes; the Wanborough temple site in Surrey produced copious quantities of silver 'minims' that occur much less frequently in presumed occupation contexts. The 'potin' coinage was widespread over most of the Home Counties and may represent a different coin usage to that served by contemporary gold coins, rather than being simply smaller denominations. A copper-alloy coinage was prolific in the North Thames region and some issues, such as the extensive range of bronzes struck by Cunobelinos, even outnumber early Roman coins on some rural sites.

Gold

Gallo-Belgic staters

Type 'A' c.125-100 BC. Struck by tribes in western France, but imported into Britain. Corresponding quarter-staters are also found.

Type 'E' c.65-55 BC. These uniface staters suggest an emergency issue associated with Caesar's Gallic War, perhaps being struck for the payment of warriors and to secure treaties.

Gallo-Belgic/British quarter stater
c.65-50 BC

'Geometric' type. There are many varieties of this quarter-stater, some uniface. The iconography has devolved from the Apollo prototype into an almost unintelligible pattern.

British uninscribed staters c.70-40 BC

There are many different types of uninscribed stater attributed to British tribal groups with discrete geographical distributions. Many are based on the Apollo head type, but with varying degrees of abstraction and evolution. Some have correspondingly similar quarter-staters.

Southern and North Thames
('Westerham' type)

Southern and North Thames
('Whaddon Chase' type)

Southern © M.R. Vosper

South-Western

South-Western - debasing into silver © M.R. Vosper

Eastern © M.R. Vosper

North-Eastern © M.R. Vosper

British uninscribed quarter-staters
c.70-40 BC

North Thames - debasing into silver

South-Eastern © CNG/M.R. Vosper

Southern

Eastern © CNG

Inscribed staters *c.40 BC - c. AD 40*

Many have correspondingly similar quarter-staters.

Commios (Southern) © Chris Rudd

Tincomaros (Southern) © Chris Rudd

Verica (Southern)

Addedomaros (N. Thames) Spiral type

Dubnovellaunos (Coins from N. Thames have an obverse wreath, those from the South-Eastern region a blank obverse)

Tasciovanos (N. Thames) Name on panel

Cunobelinos (N. Thames) Ear of barley

Corio (Western - there are several variations of this type with different names) © Chris Rudd

Bodvoc (Western) © Chris Rudd

Dumnocoveros Tigirnos Seno (N. Eastern)
© Chris Rudd

Vep Corf (N. Eastern) © M.R. Vosper

Southern & N. Thames types

Inscribed quarter-staters *c.40 BC - c. AD 40*

Tincomaros (Southern) © Chris Rudd

North Thames types- there are many varieties

Eppillos (Southern) © Chris Rudd

Eastern 'head/horse' types

Addedomaros (N. Thames)

Eastern 'boar/horse' type © Chris Rudd

Tasciovanos (N. Thames)

North-Eastern 'boar/horse' type © M.R. Vosper

Silver

Uninscribed *c.70 BC - c. AD 40*

Inscribed *c.40BC - c. AD 40*

Southern 'Danebury' type © Chris Rudd

South-Western type © Chris Rudd

Eppillos (Southern) © CNG

Western type © Chris Rudd

Verica (Southern) © CNG

14

Tasciovanos (N. Thames) - there are many
varieties

Cunobelinos (N. Thames) - there are many
varieties

Amminios (South-Eastern) © Chris Rudd

Epatticos (Southern)

Eisv (Western) © M.R. Vosper

Aun Cost (N. Eastern) © M.R. Vosper

Ecen (Eastern - there are several variations of
this type bearing different names) © CNG

Copper-Alloy

Uninscribed c.100 BC - c. AD 40

Cast 'Thurrock' type (N. Thames &
South-Eastern)

Cast 'Class 1' type (N. Thames & South-Eastern)

Southern 'Chichester Cock' type © Chris Rudd

South-Eastern type © Chris Rudd

North Thames types - there are many varieties

Cast South-Western type © M.R. Vosper

Inscribed c.40 BC - c. AD 40

Eppillos (S. Eastern) © Chris Rudd

Dubnovellaunos (S. Eastern) © Chris Rudd

Ver (N. Thames) - attributed to Tasciovanos
© M.R. Vosper

Andoco (N. Thames) © CNG

Rues (N. Thames) © CNG

*Cunobelinos (N. Thames) - there are many
varieties*

Gaulish Coins

*Coins struck by tribes in Gaul occasionally
occur as British site finds; there are many
varieties* © CNG

Contemporary forgeries

Gold-plated 'Whaddon-Chase' stater

Silver-plated unit of Cunobelinos

16

2
ROMAN COINS

Historical Background

The spread of Roman influence in western Europe brought the indigenous populations into contact with Roman culture and Roman market places, and in consequence Roman coinage. Caesar's Gallic wars included two incursions into Britain, but in AD 43 a successful landing was made under the emperor Claudius and a Roman presence established that was to last some four centuries.

Contrary to popular belief, the Roman invasion did not bring with it a massive migration of Romans. There were probably never more than around 20,000 Roman soldiers and administrators at any one time, and of these many came from other parts of the Roman Empire including Spain, Turkey and Africa. Relatively few Italians are likely to have been present. The bulk of the population remained British, and native artistic traditions continued to thrive. Although some land had been given to Roman veterans for retirement, most of the countryside continued to be farmed by native Britons, and most of the Roman 'villas' that dot the countryside were probably owned by Britons who had prospered under the new opportunities that Roman occupation afforded them. Some of these were great country houses, complete with typical Roman features such as mosaics and bath houses. In the countryside, most of the rural population probably continued to live in proximity to where they had always done, and many 'villas' overlie, or are adjacent to, Iron Age sites, of which many were probably small nucleated villages.

The Roman occupation brought with it all the symbols of 'civilisation', with the import of luxury goods and the growth of home-based industries such as metalworking and pottery production on a scale far greater than that which previously existed. All this helped to fuel a coin-based economy, with the military a major factor in the necessity of monetary supply.

The Roman occupation was not, however, a period of continual peace. Following abortive attempts to conquer Scotland, a boundary demarked by Hadrian's Wall was established, but incursions were made by northern tribes at various times, as well as localised revolts by British tribesmen and usurpations by rivals to the Imperial throne. Twice in the third century these resulted in the formation of breakaway states which included Britain. In AD 260 the commander of the legions on the Rhine, Postumus, rebelled against the Emperor Gallienus, and ruled over Gaul, Britain and Spain. This breakaway state lasted until 274, when the then ruler, Tetricus I, surrendered to the emperor Aurelian. This reunification lasted only until 286 or 287, when Carausius, the commander of the Channel Fleet, seized power in Britain and parts of Gaul. His successor Allectus was defeated by Constantius I, then Caesar, in 296. These episodes had a considerable impact upon the coinage of Britain.

In the third and fourth centuries, Britain came increasingly under attack from raiders from Ireland, Scotland and north-west Europe, and to combat this, Germanic mercenaries were employed to supplement home defence, whilst regular Roman troops were withdrawn to fight elsewhere in the Empire. In AD 407 Constantine III was proclaimed emperor by his troops in Britain, and left with much of the standing army, leaving Britain at the mercy not just of raiders, but the very mercenaries employed to defend it. In 410 the emperor Honorius wrote to the *civitates* of Britain telling them to look to their own defence, and at that point, all official contact with Rome came to an end.

The Coinage

Some of the names used by the Romans to describe their coins are known to us, others are less certain. The premier gold coin used from the time of the invasion until AD 310 was the *aureus*, with a fraction called the *quinarius*. This was replaced by the *solidus*, with its fractions the *semissis* and *tremissis*. Occasionally gold multiple denominations were produced.

The main silver coin in use until the third century was the *denarius*, being tariffed at twenty-five to the *aureus*. This likewise had a fraction, also called a *quinarius*, which is rarely found. In 215 a double *denarius* was introduced, conventionally referred to as an *antoninianus*. This had a radiate bust (wearing a crown of solar rays), rather than a laureate one, to denote its double value. *Antoniniani* gradually became debased and eventually degenerated into little barbarous copies, although the radiate type was later revived for a time. Around 295 the emperor Diocletian restored the silver coinage with a new denomination of similar fineness and weight to the *denarius* of the mid-first century. This is conventionally known as the *argenteus*. *Argentei* ceased to be struck in 308, but in around 325 two new silver coins were introduced, referred to by numismatists as the *miliarense* and the *siliqua*, which also have some very rare multiples and fractions.

The majority of Roman coins found are copper-alloy, the output of which at times was phenomenal, and unequalled until the nineteenth century. The denominations in use at the time of the Conquest were the *sestertius*, tariffed at 100 to the *aureus*, the *dupondius* (200), the *as* (400), the *semis* (800) and the *quadrans* (1600). *Dupondii* were generally struck in brass (*orichalcum*), with the emperor depicted wearing a radiate crown, whilst *asses* were generally struck in copper with the emperor wearing a laurel wreath. As mentioned, the silver radiate became debased to the point where it was effectively a copper-alloy coin, although these were 'surfaced enriched' by a

chemical process in which the surface attained a silvery appearance. Traces of this sometimes survives on excavated examples. In 274 the Emperor Aurelian carried out a monetary reform, introducing a re-tariffed radiate coin, and also issuing a new laureate bronze, conjecturally referred to as a *denarius*, being about the same size as its silver predecessor. Additionally, until the first decade of the fourth century, a few other rarely-encountered copper-alloy fractions were struck, referred to in catalogues as *quinarii, asses* and *semisses*, recalling the names of earlier issues.

In the reform of Diocletian a new large copper-alloy coin was introduced, which is listed in older publications as a *follis*. However, because we really have little idea as to what the contemporary names were of the later bronzes, it has become the convention to refer to all of them as *nummi*. *Nummus* is simply a Latin word meaning coin or money. The next major output of copper-alloy coins occurred during the reign of Constantine I, who also carried out a monetary reform. By his reign *nummi* had become reduced in size and weight. In addition to *nummi* of 20mm diameter or less, some larger bronzes were struck during the mid-4th century which are sometimes referred to as *centenionali*. Later copper-alloy issues are also referred to as Æ1s, Æ2s, Æ3s or Æ4s, depending on the size. The reason for the varying range of names is that some denominations have been mentioned in ancient documents, but numismatists are uncertain to which issues they actually refer.

The fourth century saw a huge output of *nummi* of varying types from a wide range of mints, accompanied by several widespread periods of copying, and fourth century copper-alloy coins make up the bulk of Roman site finds. In addition to the coins listed above, there were also a vast range of coins struck under the Romans in former Greek colonies and provinces. Most bear an imperial portrait but have Greek reverse types and legends. Just occasionally examples are found in Britain, and when in association with other coins of the period can be taken as being contemporary losses. Isolated finds however more probably represent post-medieval souvenirs.

During the time that Roman coins were used in Britain, the coinage itself underwent many changes in both style and denominations. Up until the early fourth century coins are best classified according to the emperor depicted, but thereafter, when several imperial colleagues often ruled, it is more relevant to classify coins, particularly bronze *nummi*, by their reverse types.

Throughout the Roman period, the coinage was subjected to continual copying, which on occasion occurred in 'epidemics'. Claudian *asses* were widely copied, presumably to meet a demand that outstripped supply. It is not certain if these copies were outright forgeries, or if produced under some official sanction. Plated *denarii* are quite common, as are cast examples, but it is the later copper-alloy coinage that is the most widely imitated. The first great epidemic occurred around AD 270, when debased radiates of the Gallic Empire were imitated with struck copies that are often very much reduced in size and very crude in style. Further epidemics occurred during the period from 330 to *c.*364. In addition to copying, many fourth century *nummi* were subjected to being cut down to produce smaller flans. This may have been with the intention of overstriking them with irregular dies, but many seem to have circulated in this reduced form.

With illegible Roman base metal coins, size and metal colour can provide clues to attribution. Large base metal coins of the first to early third centuries were struck in both copper and brass. Coins from the late third century onwards generally have a brassy look, apart from the Valentinianic period (364-378) when many excavated examples exhibit a distinctive coppery colour with a corresponding lighter green patination. This, taken together with flan size and weight and vestigial design details can often allow coins of this period to be correctly attributed. Very

occasionally, illegible coins may be found that approximate in size to copper coins of the late seventeenth and eighteenth centuries. Just as the flan profile can be used to distinguish between Iron Age and Roman small bronzes, so too can it indicate whether a coin is Roman or post-medieval. The following illustration shows how a Roman coin that has been subject to surface corrosion and subsequent metal loss differs in profile from a milled coin that will not have been subjected to the same type of corrosion, resulting in a much squarer rim profile.

(a) Roman coin   *(b) milled coin*

Site Finds

The Roman invasion led to an influx of Roman coins current at the time, and throughout the period, huge numbers of coins were used within the Roman-controlled parts of Britain. The coins fed a market economy that was probably closely related to the economic needs of the Army, which required a large civilian infrastructure to support it. Many Roman towns grew up around early military camps. The types of coin used in Britain usually originated from mints in Western Europe, although in some periods coins were struck in London and possibly at other mints in the country.

Studies of Roman coin lists from sites in Britain suggest two distinct types of assemblage, one predominating on military and urban sites, the other on rural civilian sites. Statistical research has also suggested that the types of coins being used within towns can differ from the types of coins turning up outside. However, since much of the early data are based on conventionally excavated coins rather than on controlled metal detecting evidence, it is almost certainly under-representative and thus statistically unsound and needs to be viewed with some circumspection. What finds do suggest is that in the southern part of the province there was a much more active market economy, which is reflected in the coins used and thus lost.

Roman coin supply to Britain does not seem to have been consistent, with sporadic influxes of new coins followed by periods of minimal supply. That there was no shortage of coins in general is evidenced by large assemblages recovered from sites such as Coventina's Well on Hadrian's Wall, and the sacred spring at Bath, where coins struck before AD 260 actually outnumber later ones even though, at Bath at any rate, the use of the site does not seem to have declined post-AD 260. This is not however reflected on rural sites, where pre-AD 260 coins often represent less than 10% of the total assemblage. Even amongst this 10%, most early copper-alloy coins exhibit considerable wear, suggesting that they did not arrive in the countryside until the third century. Unworn *Sestertii* are extremely rare as rural finds. It would seem from this that some significant social or economic event brought about a need for a rural cash economy that had not previously existed, occurring around the time of the formation of the breakaway empire of Postumus. One explanation for this might be connected with the military.

Archaeological research indicates that during the third century, towns were provided with improved defensive systems whilst at the same time experiencing a decline in the construction of new public works. This is juxtaposed by the expansion of rural 'villa' sites, often with the addition of bath houses. This suggests that the ruling elite were forsaking towns for rural estates, but ensuring that the towns were defendable should the need to seek sanctuary arise. This broadly coincides with internecine fighting within the Roman Empire by various imperial contenders, opportunistic attacks by barbarian tribes, and a corresponding reduction of established trading markets. The Roman army, now contracted, was reorganised into a more mobile force which instead of maintaining rigid lines of defence seems to have been more reliant on 'elastic defence', per-

haps using cavalry patrols or 'flying columns' based as much in rural as in urban locations. This much we broadly know from history, and thus the sudden upsurge in rural coin loss, accompanied by Roman military fittings that occur with frequency on many sites, must surely be confirmation of these changed circumstances.

Of the coins themselves, nearly six hundred Roman gold coins are recorded as single finds in Britain, but this still makes them extremely rare in relation to the millions of copper-alloy coins that have been found. Their distribution pattern is also different from silver and copper-alloy. A significant number of *aurei* have been found in the military zones of Britain, such as the lowlands of Scotland, Wales and Cornwall, and there is a peak of *aurei* of the Emperor Nero, particularly the 'Juppiter Custos' reverse which was struck circa AD 64-5 to honour Jupiter for protecting the Emperor from the Pisonian conspiracy. It is possible that a large issue was produced as a reward to those troops who remained loyal to the emperor, and that these coins remained largely within the military economy. Soldiers may have retained some of them as their retirement 'nest eggs'. Some of the finds may be concealed *aurei* belonging to troops who failed to survive a particular emergency such as one of the frequent raids by the Scots. *Solidi*, often of the emperors Honorius and Arcadius, occur more widely, and may reflect the political troubles of the late Roman period, with the coins perhaps being used to pay for mercenaries, or as bribes to keep troops and local potentates loyal

Silver *denarii* occur with some frequency, and include many forgeries, both plated and cast. Worn *denarii* of the Republic continued to circulate well into the Imperial period. The silver *'argentei'* of Carausius are scarce but not infrequent finds, although the silver issues of his rivals do not seem to have reached Britain. The *miliarense* likewise seems to have had little British circulation, and most recovered in Britain have derived from hoards, often with *Siliquae,* which clearly did circulate as individual coins of exchange. *Siliquae* are in fact fairly common, but are often found with metal from their outer circumferences clipped away. This may represent weight adjustment, or the removal of silver for nefarious purposes, which was a common practice in the medieval and early post-medieval periods.

Copper-alloy *sestertii, dupondii* and *asses* are frequently found, although both *semisses* and *quadrantes* are rare site finds in Britain, and then only normally in urban contexts. The breakaway empires referred to above are reflected in the coins that are found. The first action of any new ruler in Roman times was usually to strike a new coinage proclaiming his supremacy, but coins of Postumus, mainly base silver radiates and sestertii, are relatively scarce as British site finds. Conversely, the coins of his rival, Gallienus, are comparatively common, particularly those of his sole reign which post-date AD 260. This begs the question why, if Britain had declared for Postumus, are Postumus's coins significantly outnumbered by those of Gallienus when occurring as site finds? One answer could be that most coins of Gallienus's joint reign and those of Postumus contained a greater percentage of silver than those of Gallienus's sole reign, and thus were hoarded rather than circulated. But this still does not explain the presence of coins of Gallienus who, if history is correct, was ruling a separate and hostile territory. It is also unlikely that they were imported after the re-conquest of the west by Aurelian as it is the coins of Postumus's successors that were by then dominant, and it is their coins that were extensively copied as 'barbarous radiates'. Few copies of Gallienus's coins are found. The most likely conclusion therefore must be that history has been misinterpreted, and that at least part of Britain remained within the sphere of governance of the Central Empire until the reign of Victorinus, whose coins, together with those of the Tetrici, are prolific and extensively copied. The defeat of the Tetrici by Aurelian

in AD 274 did not bring a flood of Aurelianic coinage into the rural currency pool. Instead it is coins of his predecessor, Claudius II that dominate, particularly copies of the commemorative types struck after his death. Why this should be is unclear, but it may be that the legions that re-established central control in Britain brought with them a pool of Claudian coin, not Aurelianic. Given that the Tetrici were pardoned by Aurelian, it may be that their coins were allowed to continue to circulate, rather than being proscribed. Although large numbers of Aurelianic radiates are known from hoards, few seem to have circulated to be lost as site finds, and it may be that they were over-valued. Whatever the reason, from *c.*274 to 287, there was a massive output in both Britain and Gaul of imitative copies of coins then current, predominately those of the Tetrici and Claudius II. These are frequently very crude and often tiny. A substantial output of radiates was also produced by the breakaway emperor Carausius, and his successor Allectus. Some issues of Carausius are also very crude and probably initially utilised the talents of the 'barbarous radiate' die-cutters, but others, probably later ones, are of good weight and style, and these are fairly common as British site finds.

Nummi from the reform of Diocletian are also frequently found, early examples being much less common than later ones; by the end of the reign of Constantine I *nummi*, by now reduced in size to 18mm or less, are even more prolific than radiates, and again a significant number found are irregular copies. As the fourth century progressed, there were several phases of copper-alloy issues which occur with regularity in Britain. These include a new coinage of *nummi* struck after 348, large bronzes struck under Magnentius and Decentius, a large output of *nummi* of around 18mm. between 364 and 378, and at the very end of the Roman period, small *nummi* struck between 388 and 402. It is interesting to note that some of these latter coins exhibit considerable wear, suggesting a continuing use well into the fifth century, although in what capacity they were used we do not know.

Illegible coins: A considerable number of Roman coins that occur as field finds are frequently totally illegible or fragmentary, but even so every single one should be plotted and recorded as they are all of statistical value, even if they can only be placed into a very broad date range based on size alone.

In the following list, all dates shown in parentheses are *Anno Domini* unless otherwise stated, followed by reverse type and mint where relevant.

Gold

Aureus of Nero (54-68) Salus © CNG

Aureus of Galerius, (305-11) Jupiter, Trier

Solidus of Valentinian I (364-75) Valentinian and Valens enthroned, Trier © CNG

Solidus of Arcadius (395-402) Emperor trampling enemy, Ravenna

Silver

Denarii

L. Flaminius Chilo (109-8 BC) © CNG

Julius Caesar (48-7 BC) trophy © CNG

Marcus Antonius (d.30 BC) legionary issue © CNG

Augustus (27 BC - AD14)
Caius & Lucius Caesars © CNG

Tiberius (14-37) ?Pax © CNG

Nero (54-68) Jupiter © CNG

Vespasian (69-79) Judea © CNG

Domitian (81-96) Minerva

Trajan (98-117) Abundantia

Hadrian (117-38) Roma

Antoninus Pius (138-61) Roma

Faustina Senior (d.141) Vesta

Marcus Aurelius (161-80) Emperor standing

Faustina Junior (d.175) Fecunditas © CNG

Septimius Severus (193-211) Apollo

Julia Domna (d.217) Pietas

Antoninus 'Caracalla' (198-217) Liberalitas

Antoninus 'Elagabalus' (218-22) Roma

Severus Alexander (222-35) Mars

Julia Mamaea (d.235) Juno

Maximinus I (235-8) emperor between standards

'Argenteus'

Carausius (287-93) Wolf & Twins, 'RSR' mint

Radiates

Gordian III (238-44) Providentia © CNG

Valerian I (253-60) Virtus © CNG

Gallienus (253-68) Virtus © CNG

Salonina (d.268) Venus

Postumus (259-68) Emperor standing

'Miliarense'

Valens (364-78) Emperor with standard, Trier
© CNG

'Siliquae'

Constantius II (337-61) Vota, Arles © CNG

Julian II (360-3) Vota, Lyons

Valens (364-78) Roma, Trier © CNG

Gratian (367-83) Roma, Trier

Arcadius (383-408) Roma, Trier

Copper-Alloy

Sestertii

Trajan (97-117) Pax © CNG

Marcus Aurelius (161-80) M. Aurelius and L. Verus © CNG

Hadrian (117-38) Felicitas © CNG

Commodus (177-92) Mars © CNG

Antoninus Pius (138-61) Honus © CNG

Severus Alexander (222-35) Providentia

Faustina Senior (d. 141) Aeternitas

Postumus - double sestertius (260-9) emperor standing © CNG

Dupondii *Usually brass with a radiate crown on male busts*

Asses *Usually copper with laureate bust*

Antonia (41-54) Claudius © CNG

Germanicus (d. 19) SC © CNG

Nero (54-68) Victory - laureate issue of Lyons

Domitian (81-96) Moneta

Vespasian (69-79) Victory © CNG

Vespasian (69-79) Aequitas

Trajan (97-117) emperor spearing Dacian © CNG

Trajan (98-117) Victory

Hadrian (117-38) Emperor and Roma © CNG

Hadrian (117-38) Salus

Antoninus Pius (138-61) Britannia

Lucilla (d. 182) Vesta © CNG

Otacilia Severa (244-9) Concordia © CNG

Semis

Nero (54-68) Vase and wreath on table

'Denarius'

Aurelian (270-5) Victory © CNG

Radiates

Gallienus (260-8) Antelope © CNG

Claudius II (268-70) Fides © CNG

Victorinus (268-70) Pax

Tetricus I (270-3) Hilaritas

Tetricus II (270-3) Spes

Aurelian (270-5) Concordia © M. R. Vosper

Probus (276-82) Minerva © CNG

Victories resting shield (318-9) Constantine I,
Siscia © M.R. Vosper

Carausius (287-93) Pax, London

Captives and standard (320-1) Constantine I,
London © CNG

Allectus (293-6) Galley, 'C' mint

Altar (320-4) Constantine II, London

Nummi AD 294 -330

Genius (294-316) Maximianus, Lyons

Vota in wreath (320-4) Constantine I,
Thessalonica

Sol (307-19) Constantine I, Lyons

Sarmatia (323-5) Constantine I, Trier

Securitas (324-5) Helena, Thessalonica © CNG

Sol half unit (307-19) Constantine I, Trier

Gateway (324-30) Crispus, Trier

Nummi AD 330-48

Many contemporary copies exist. Official issues of 330-5 should fall within the weight and size parameters of 1.9-2.8 grammes and 16-18mm. Those of 335-48 should be 1.2 grammes or above and 14-16mm. Any coins below these ranges are probably copies.

Victory on prow (330-5) Trier

Wolf and Twins (330-5) Trier

Two soldiers and two standards (330-5) Constantine I, Arles

Two soldiers and one standard (335-41) Constantius II, Lyons

Pax (337-41) Helena, Trier

Pietas (337-41) Theodora, Trier

Emperor in quadriga (337-41) Constantine I, Trier

Star in wreath (341-8) Constantinople

Bridge (341-8) Constantinople

Two Victories (347-8) Constans, Trier

Nummi AD 348 - 64

Emperor on galley (348-50) Constantius II, Trier
© CNG

Soldier dragging captive from hut (348-50) Constans, Trier

Phoenix (348-50) Constans, Trier

Chi-Rho (350-3) Magnentius, Trier © M.R. Vosper

Emperor and standard (350-53) Magnentius, Trier

Horseman spearing enemy (350-3) Magnentius, Trier

Two victories (350-3) Magnentius, Lyons

Fallen horseman (348-54) Constantius II, Lyons - fallen Horseman coins less than 4.75g and 22mm are probably irregular, and these made up the bulk of the coinage for the rest of the period up until 364.

Nummi AD 364 - 78

Emperor dragging captive, Valens, Siscia © CNG

Victory, Valentinian I, Siscia

Emperor with standard, Gratian, Arles (this type was only issued for this emperor at this mint)

Nummi AD 378 - 402

Vota in wreath (378-83) Gratian, Arles © CNG

Gateway (387-8) Flavius Victor, Aquileia © CNG

Victory with wreath (388-402) Arcadius, Lyons

Victory dragging captive (388-402) Valentinian II, Aquileia © CNG

Irregular coins

'Claudius I' Minerva © CNG

Octavian (Augustus) plated denarius

Antoninus 'Caracalla' plated denarius

Radiates (struck c.270-84)

'Claudius II'

'Tetricus I'

'Tetricus II'

'minim'

Nummi (struck c.340-8)

Wolf and Twins

Soldiers and standards

Virtus

Nummi (struck c.350-64)

'Magnentius'

Fallen horseman © M.R. Vosper

Fallen horseman (overstruck on an earlier coin)

Reduced flan coins

Cut-down fallen horseman

Cut-down 'Chi-Rho'

3
MEDIEVAL COINS

Historical Background

The Middle Ages are generally defined as the period between the fall of the Western Roman Empire and the Renaissance. For British coins, the Renaissance first manifests itself with the coinage of James III in Scotland (1460-88), and Henry VII in England (1485-1509). Both reigns saw the introduction of new realistic portraiture on groats in Scotland and both groats and testoons in England.

Details of the transition to Anglo-Saxon England are historically obscure, leading to the term 'Dark Ages' for the early part of the period. Traditional accounts such as that of Bede, writing some centuries after the events he described, are now looked upon as oversimplistic and in part fictitious. Written accounts are few and archaeological evidence generally sparse, but the most likely scenario is that Germanic and possibly Irish mercenaries replaced Roman troops for home defence purposes, and then ousted local civil government with a 'warlord' structure. This probably resulted in 'ethnic cleansing' in some areas, subjugation in others, and quite possibly peaceful co-existence and cultural absorption elsewhere. All of the material trappings of Roman society, including coinage, disappeared and for the first few centuries following the collapse of Roman rule masonry buildings were eschewed for timber, and goods such as pottery and brooches seemed to have been mainly confined to funerary use. In many places, whoever the population were, they are now archaeologically invisible.

The emergence of modern Britain from the Dark Ages involved the growth of Saxon kingdoms which developed from small units into larger ones such as Wessex and Mercia, and these ultimately merged to form England. From the eighth century, England was subject to raids and settlement from Danish and Norse invaders, and in 1016 the Danish King Canute became King of England. In 1066 Duke William of Normandy successfully wrested the throne from the last Saxon king, Harold II. This event linked the destiny of England to France and paved the way for centuries of territorial conflict. In 1135, on the death of Henry I, Civil war broke out, which at its conclusion left Stephen de Blois King of England. During the reign of King John, much English territory in France was lost, and civil unrest continued with John warring with some of his barons. War with France dominated much of the fourteenth and fifteenth centuries, as did plague in the form of the Black Death, which swept Europe in 1348. Up to a third of the population of Britain was wiped out, but from this depopulation there emerged a new and stronger yeoman class, and the latter part of the Middle Ages was a time of relative prosperity.

As with early England, Wales and Scotland also grew from smaller kingdoms. Wales remained independent of England until conquered by Edward I in the thirteenth century, and thereafter was regarded as a principality. Scotland, despite intermittent warfare and military incursions across the English border by both sides, managed to maintain its independence from England throughout the medieval period.

In Europe things were somewhat different, and the new rulers of the western Roman Empire adopted much of the existing Roman culture. The Roman Empire in the east, or Byzantine Empire, based on Constantinople, continued until the fifteenth century, when it fell to the Ottoman Turks. Europe was, for much of the Middle Ages, made up of small states and principalities, and it was not until the eighteenth and nineteenth centuries that many of the nations that now comprise modern Europe began to form.

The Coinage

The reappearance of a monetary system in Britain occurred in the late sixth to early seventh century, when European gold coins began to be imported, followed by an English series of gold and later silver pieces. The gold coins derive from the *tremissis*, a Roman denomination of one third of a *solidus,* and are conventionally known as *thrymsas*. These became increasingly debased and eventually evolved into silver pennies, which are popularly referred to by numismatists as *'sceattas'*, meaning treasure or wealth. They were produced in silver until around the end of the eighth century in southern England, and continued in copper-alloy in Northumbria until around the middle of the ninth century. These latter are conventionally termed *'stycas'*, although they are nothing more than debased pennies that presumably had a local token value. Site finds suggest that Merovingian and Frisian coins circulated alongside English ones and in some cases, as with the so-called 'porcupine' types, it is not always possible to say with certainty where they originated. The 'porcupines' seem to have been a common currency both sides of the North Sea and for this reason they are grouped together in this book under English coins.

In the eighth century, the various kingdoms of Saxon England began to produce pennies based on the new broader flan deniers of the Franks. The broad flan penny continued as the only denomination until the thirteenth century, when other types of coin were introduced.

The earlier Saxon broad flan pennies are very varied in types, having sometimes lines of legend on both sides, or obverse busts and reverse legends or motifs of various kinds. Later ones commonly have an obverse bust and a cross of some sort on the reverse, along with the name of the mint and moneyer. The Norman Conquest did little to alter the appearance of the coinage in any significant way. From 1158 all portraits are depicted full face, and from 1180 became quite immobilised in style. Later Saxon and Norman period coins were struck at a great number of different locations around the country, usually under the auspices of local entrepreneurs who, acting as moneyers, underwrote the quality of the coins. Most dies would have been engraved in London and transported to workshops under the control of the moneyers, who did not have any actual physical involvement in the striking of the coins.

The penny remained the main medium of coinage until the reign of Edward I. Although a few very scarce round halfpennies and farthings were struck in the previous reign, fractions had been achieved by cutting pennies into halves and quarters (literally 'halfpenny' and 'fourthling' or farthing). These cut fractions are very common finds, with cut halves outnumbering whole pence or farthings. Cut halves of Saxon and Norman broad-flan pennies occur occasionally before the introduction of the voided 'short cross' coins of 1180, and some 'Tealby' pennies were quartered for farthings, but only after 1180 did the practice of halving and quartering become commonplace, ceasing with the new coinage of Edward I. The practice seems to be specific to England, and seems to be virtually unknown in other countries. For example, in France at the time, round *obols*, a half unit of the standard *denier*, were struck in considerable numbers, but do not seem to occur cut into quarter units.

Reference was made in the last chapter to the clipping of coins. It was a common practice to remove small shavings from the edges of coins and to retain them for their silver value, sometimes using the metal to strike underweight forgeries. Frequent attempts were made to curtail the practice, but it continued right through until the end of the hammered coinage. Sometimes coins will be found that appear to be clipped, but are in fact the correct weight, and were simply struck on small flans.

In 1279, Edward introduced a new coin, a four penny piece known as the groat. This issue was short-lived, and it took until 1344 for a new range of denominations to be introduced. These comprised a very limited production of gold pieces based on the florin, a gold noble and its fractions, and silver groats, half-groats, pennies, halfpennies and farthings. This remained unchanged throughout the remaining medieval period, other than the introduction of two new gold denominations, the ryal and the angel, during the reign of Edward IV.

Other than a very rare penny issued by the Welsh king Howel Dda around AD 950, Wales has never had an independent national coinage, with English coinage being used when necessary. Until the twelfth century Scotland likewise had no coinage of its own, but following the capture of the mint town of Carlisle by David I in 1136, a coinage was commenced following the pattern of the English coinage, comprising pennies and later round halfpennies and farthings, all with profile busts. In 1357 David II introduced the noble, groat and halfgroat to Scotland, and Robert III established a gold coinage consisting of the lion and demy-lion, which approximated to English half and quarter nobles. Robert III also introduced a facing bust, similar in style to those used on the English coinage. His reign also saw a debasement of pennies and halfpennies take place.

James III (1460-88) introduced new gold denominations, the rider and the unicorn, and for the first time a new three-quarters facing bust was used on the groat, although the medieval-style facing bust continued to be used for some time on other denominations. Also used for the first time was the thistle emblem. Base pennies and halfpennies continued; a distinctive base fourpence known as a plack was struck, as were regal copper-alloy farthings (referred to as 'black money') and a group of copper-alloy pennies and farthings of possible ecclesiastical origin, conjecturally issued by Bishop James Kennedy of St. Andrews.

Site Finds

Following the collapse of the Roman Imperial administration in Britain, the use of coins seems to have ceased. It was once suggested that the small irregular issues referred to in the last chapter were 'sub-Roman' issues struck in the fifth century, but that has now been discounted. Roman coins may still have had a bullion value, and some may have been used as weights. Occasional finds of early Byzantine coins may represent contemporary losses in this context, but many are more likely to be from burials or later souvenirs.

The first coins of the post-Roman period that occur as contemporary site finds are occasional Merovingian *tremisses* and *deniers*, and their English equivalents, the *'thrymsas'* and *'sceattas'*. These latter occur in sufficient numbers as to suggest that by the early eighth century there was once again a significant coin-based market economy. With the introduction of the broad flan penny in the late eighth century this changed, and single finds of coins from then until the introduction of the 'short-cross' penny in 1180 are comparatively rare. This may reflect a change in market circumstances and/or coin distribution, or simply an undersupply of coinage, the shortfall possibly being met by barter. It is clear that the short cross coinage was of a greater output than the preceding 'Tealby' coinage, but how much greater has yet to be established. Whatever the commercial reasons behind the output increase, it clearly filled a need that had not been adequately met before, and the fractions in particular make interesting statistics.

Documentary and hoard evidence can reveal much about the coins being struck, but little about their use. Metal detector finds however reflect a truer picture of what was going on in the market place. Although a few round halfpence and farthings of the short cross coinage have been found, nearly all known fractions are round pennies that have been sheared into halves and quarters. Based on a sample of 133 metal-detected coins

34

(excluding Scottish and Irish), the following percentages were noted. Voided Short Cross: Whole coins 28%, cut halves 57% and cut farthings 15%. Voided Long Cross: Whole coins 27%, cut halves 69% and cut farthings 4%. This is remarkably similar to other surveys. I did consider the possibility that the statistics might be affected by cut farthings being more difficult to detect, but field tests demonstrated that both halves and quarters have similar conductivity when buried. This clearly indicates that halfpennies were the commonest denomination by choice, and thus must have accommodated a particular commodity or service prevalent at the time. Following on from the voided cross coinages, the new Edwardian sterling coinage, together with round halfpence and farthings, are quite common finds.

Groats occasionally turn up, including the rare issues of Edward I. These latter normally show evidence of having been gilded and converted into brooches, and so do not represent monetary use and loss. Most coin finds are of halfgroats and lesser denominations, and this continues to be the case throughout the medieval period. However, a significant number of gold coins have been found, with a number of full nobles being recorded. Some of these seem to have been deliberately bent or rolled into cylinders, perhaps representing a means of carrying them as bullion. Enough nobles and their fractions have been found singly to suggest that they did play a part in a cash economy.

During the later medieval period many English coins circulated in Scotland and vice-versa, but Scottish finds all but cease in England with Robert III's debasement. Until then, Scottish and English coins had been of the same weight and thus value, and both circulated either side of the border. In Scotland, finds of coins of Richard I to Edward II are not unusual, but cease with Edward III and only recommence with the Tudors. In England finds run from David I to Robert II, with William the Lion and Alexander III being the most prolific.

Ireland was conquered by the English in the twelfth century, and coins were struck there sporadically. Many Irish pennies were produced during the reigns of Henry III and Edward I, and a great number found their way to Britain. A hiatus of coining occurred in the fourteenth and fifteenth centuries, but recommenced in earnest during the reign of Edward IV, with pennies again being occasional finds in Britain. Some groats of Henry VI were clipped back to form two denominations, a half groat with the inner reverse legend showing and a penny clipped back right to the inner circles; even plated forgeries of such sheared coins were made. England retained possessions in France until the loss of Calais in the sixteenth century. Calais mint coins are stylistically the same as those struck in England, but coins of Aquitaine and Poitou are of a distinctive style, and occasionally occur as finds in Britain.

Other foreign coins turn up with some frequency in British soil. Many no doubt arrived through trade, but some may have been souvenirs of pilgrimages or crusades and others more recent tourist imports. On occasion foreign coins have circulated, either with or without official sanction, particularly in times of short supply of small change. Arab *dirhems* have been found in some numbers, both in hoards and singularly, and often as fragments. They are clearly associated with Viking activity and represent bullion rather than currency. French gold *ecus* circulated on a par with English coins, and Florentine *fiorini* are known to have been used. Other European gold coins occasionally occur. Double *patards* of Brabant and Burgundy were accepted as legal tender and circulated as groats until the sixteenth century. Venetian *soldini* also circulated spasmodically in an unofficial capacity. In addition, during the thirteenth and fourteenth centuries, there was a prolific output of sterlings from the Low Countries, struck in imitation of English coins. Some copies of Edwardian type are known as pollards' or 'crockards'; these have a bare-headed bust or a rosette diadem in place of a crown, and give the name of the issuing duke and the mint. Some, however, are close copies of the English prototype and only differ in stylistic details. Unlike England and Scotland, which had coinages unified under one monarch, the coinages of many European countries were produced by ecclesiastical bodies or dukes and local potentates, in addition to national rulers, leading to a huge diversity of variation and types.

English Coins

Gold

'Thrymsas' (c.600-70) © M.R. Vosper

Edward III (1344-77) noble

Henry V (1413-22) quarter noble © CNG

Edward IV (1461-83) angel

Silver *(unless otherwise indicated)*

Certain medieval coins were subject to debasement, and just a few were struck in copper-alloy. Most however in this period were silver

Small-flan Pennies c. AD 670-850

These are classified into a range of groups and sub-groups of great complexity and varied style, and the whole series is now in need of reclassification. Some types within series 'C' and 'R' are variations of the bust/standard type of series 'A'. One variety of series 'J' is a regional variation of series 'B'.

On some coins, the prototype Roman profile bust became reduced to an abstract image commonly referred to as a 'porcupine', which eventually became an icon in its own right and even appeared as a reverse image paired with a more conventional obverse bust.

Series 'A' Bust/standard

Series 'B' Bust/bird on cross

Series 'D' Cross/standard

Series 'E' 'Porcupine' bust/standard

Series 'F' Bust/stepped cross

Series 'H' Face in pellet annulets/fantastic bird
© M.R. Vosper

Series 'T' Wolf and twins/displayed bird

Series 'J' Two heads vis-a-vis/cross and birds © CNG

Series 'X' Face/fantastic beast © CNG

Series 'K' Bust/serpent © M.R. Vosper

Series 'Z' Face/quadruped © M.R. Vosper

Series 'M' Quadruped/foliate motif © M.R. Vosper

Northumbria, Eadberht © CNG

Series 'N' Two standing 'emperors'/fantastic beast © M.R. Vosper

Northumbria, Æ Archbishop Wigmund © M.R. Vosper

Broad-flan Pennies from the 8th to 10th Centuries AD

Series 'O' Bust/serpent © CNG

Mercia, Offa (757-96) © CNG

Series 'Q' Quadruped/bird © CNG

Kent, Wulfred (805-32) © CNG

Series 'S' Sphinx/whorl of wolf-heads

East Anglia, Edmund (855-70) Imitative issue
© M.R. Vosper

Wessex, Alfred (871-899) Canterbury © CNG

York, Cnut (c.898-915) © CNG

Edgar (959-975) York © CNG

English Pennies AD 975-1180

Aethelred II (978-1016) 'last small cross' type, Maldon

Cnut (1016-35) 'quatrefoil' type, Oxford © CNG

Harold I (1035-40) 'jewel cross' type, Colchester

Edward the Confessor (1042-66) 'trefoil quadrilateral' type, York © CNG

Harold II (1066) 'Pax' type, Lewes © CNG

William I (1066-87) 'two stars' type, London

William II (1087-1100) 'Cross in quatrefoil' type, Norwich

Henry I (1100-35) 'annulets and piles' type, Exeter

Stephen (1135-54) 'Watford' type, London

Henry II (1154-89) 'Tealby' type, Newcastle © CNG

Cut halfpenny and cut farthing

English Coins 12th to 16th Centuries

Henry II (1154-89) penny, Northampton

Edward I (1279-1307) groat, London

Richard I (1189-99) penny, London

Edward I penny, London

John (1199-1216) penny, Exeter

Edward I halfpenny, London

Edward I farthing, London

Henry III (1216-72) 'short-cross' penny, London

Edward II (1301-27) penny, Canterbury

*Henry III 'long-cross' penny,
Canterbury*

Edward II halfpenny, London

39

Edward II farthing, London

Edward III (1327-77) groat, London

Edward III halfgroat, London

Edward III penny, London

Edward III halfpenny, London

Edward III farthing, London

Richard II (1377–99) halfgroat, London

Richard II penny, York

Richard II halfpenny, London

Richard II farthing, London © CNG

Henry IV (1399-1413) halfgroat, London

Henry IV penny, London

Henry IV halfpenny, London

Henry V (1413-22) groat, London

Henry V halfgroat, London

Henry V penny, London

Henry V halfpenny, London

Henry VI (1422-61) groat, Calais

Henry VI halfgroat, Calais

Henry VI penny, Calais © CNG

Henry VI halfpenny, London

Edward IV (1461-83) groat, London

Edward IV halfgroat, Canterbury

Edward IV penny, Durham

Edward IV halfpenny, London

Richard III (1483-5) groat, London

Richard III penny, Durham

Henry VII (1485-1509) groat, London © CNG

John Baliol (1292-6) halfpenny © Spink

Henry VII halfgroat, Canterbury

Henry VII facing bust penny, York © Galata

David II (1329-71) groat, Edinburgh © CNG

Henry VII halfpenny, London

Scottish Coins, 12th to 16th Centuries
Gold

David II penny, Edinburgh © CNG

James IV (1488-1513) unicorn © CNG

Robert II (1371-90) halfgroat, Edinburgh

Silver *(unless otherwise indicated)*

William I (1165-1214) penny

James III (1460-88) groat, Edinburgh © CNG

Alexander III (1249-86) penny

James III new style groat, Edinburgh © CNG

James III Æ 'Bishop Kennedy' penny

James IV (1488-1513) penny, Edinburgh © CNG

Medieval coins from overseas found in Britain *(silver unless otherwise indicated)*

Denmark

Erik VII of Pomerania (1396-1439) sterling (struck in both silver and copper)

France

Merovingian gold tremissis (c. 570-670)

Merovingian denier (c. 670-750)

Louis the Pious (814-40) denier © M.R. Vosper

Valence (12th-13th century) denier

Louis IX (1245-70) denier tournois

Aquitaine, Prince Edward (1253-73) denier au lion

Philippe IV (1285-1314) denier tournois

Brittany, Jean III (1312-41) denier

Charles IV (1322-8) maille blanche

Philippe VI (1328-50) gros tournois

Charles VI (1380-1422) gold écu d'or

Charles VI blanc

Brittany, Jean V (1399-1442) blanc

Germany

*Cologne, Archbishop Philip of Heinsberg
(1167-8) pfennig*

*Teutonic Order, Winrich von Kniprode or
Conrad (1351-90) vierling*

*Teutonic Order, Paul von Russdorf (1422-41)
schilling*

*Trier, Archbishop Johann II (1456-1503)
weissgroschen*

Ireland

Prince John (1189-99) halfpenny, Dublin © CNG

John (1207-11) penny, Dublin © M.R. Vosper

Henry III (1216-72) penny, Dublin

Edward I (1272-1307) penny, Dublin

Edward I halfpenny, Dublin © CNG

Edward IV (1461-83) penny, Dublin

Edward IV penny, Trim

Islamic

*Abbasids, Haroun al Rashid (AD788-809)
dirhem*

Italy

Pavia, Otto I or II (961-84) denaro

Lucca, Conrad II (1024-39) denaro

Genoa (1139-1339) denaro

Bologna, (15th century) grosso

Venice, Tomaso Mocenigo (1413-23) soldino

Venice, Francesco Foscari (1423-57) ducato

Low Countries

Voided long-cross sterling copy (13th century)

Brabant, Henry II-III (1235-61) petit denier

Brabant, Jean II (1276-1302) sterling

Holland, Floris V (1256-96) denier

Flanders, Bruges (13th century), petit denier

*Looz, Arnold V (1279-1323)
sterling ('pollard')*

Hainault, John of Avesnes (1290-5)
sterling ('crockard')

Flanders & Namur, Gui de Dampierre
(1279-1305) sterling ('crockard')

Flanders & Namur, Robert de Béthune
(1305-22) sterling

Florennes, Gaucher de Châtillon (1313-22)
sterling

Namur & Méraude, William of Namur
(1337-91) sterling

Anonymous sterling in the name of Edward of
England (14th century)

Brabant, Charles the Bold (1467-77)
double patard

Portugal

Alfonso V (1438-81) chinfrão

Alfonso V Æ ceitil

John II (1481-95) vintem

Spain

Ferdinand & Isabella (1497-1516) real

Ferdinand & Isabella half-real

4
EARLY POST-MEDIEVAL COINS

Historical Background

The European Renaissance is taken as marking the end of the medieval period. Numismatically it was a period of great diversity of new denominations, and heralded the transition from the production of coins by hand to the use of mechanical means. For this reason it is perhaps appropriate to examine coins struck during Tudor and Stuart times as a separate category.

At the close of the fifteenth century, Britain remained divided into two kingdoms, England and Scotland. At this time England was still a small European state, with no overseas territories save Ireland and a tenuous toehold in France, the latter ending with the capture of Calais by the Duke of Guise in 1558. The sixteenth century saw much of Europe in turmoil, with religious conflict between the established church of Rome and new doctrines such as Lutheranism, aided and abetted by the development of the printing press. The first major schism for England came with Henry VIII's rejection of Rome, and the establishment of the Church of England. Mary Tudor sought to reverse this both through her marriage with King Philip of Spain, and her persecution of Protestants. Her policies were in turn reversed by her successor Elizabeth I, who re-established the Protestant faith, and successfully defeated an invasion attempt by Spain which was aimed at re-establishing a Catholic monarchy. It was during Elizabeth's reign that Scotland became once more entwined with England's destiny, her queen, Mary, becoming a prisoner of the English and ultimately being executed by Elizabeth. The final irony of the convoluted politics of the time was that Mary's son James succeeded the childless Elizabeth to become king of both Scotland and England, and thus in effect the first king of Britain.

The sixteenth century saw the first beginnings of British imperial expansion, with adventurers such as Drake and Raleigh venturing to America, and the migration there in the seventeenth century of colonists who set out to establish new lives. The reign of Charles I saw Britain embroiled in a series of civil wars, culminating in the king's execution and the establishment of a republic under Oliver Cromwell. In 1660 Charles II returned from exile, and the monarchy was restored.

The Coinage

England

The accession to the English throne of Henry Tudor as Henry VII in 1485 brought with it a departure from the immobilised coinage of the later Middle Ages. A new gold piece of twenty shillings, the sovereign, was introduced, and on the silver coinage the traditional facing bust penny was replaced by one depicting the king enthroned in the style of the sovereign, and the newly fashionable Renaissance style of portraiture was introduced on a new denomination, the testoon, a very rare coin tariffed at twelve pence. On this, and on groats and halfgroats, the king is depicted in profile. Henry's son, Henry VIII, introduced some new gold pieces known as the George Noble, Crown of the Rose and Crown of the Double Rose. There was also a gold halfcrown. Henry VIII's silver coins continued with profile bust groats and halfgroats and the 'sovereign' type penny. Halfpennies continued in the medieval facing bust style, but a new and tiny round farthing was also introduced. In 1544 Henry struck a new series of silver coins with a distinctive facing bust, which continued to be produced in the early years of Edward VI's reign, but now struck in debased silver. Coins depicting Edward in profile were struck from 1549 to

1551, the later ones being very debased, but these were replaced by a new fine silver coinage which introduced for the first time a silver five shilling piece, the crown, and a corresponding halfcrown. A new facing bust appeared on shillings, sixpences and threepences.

Edward's successor Mary Tudor, who for a time ruled jointly with her husband Philip of Spain, discontinued the crown and halfcrown, but struck some distinctive shillings and sixpences depicting both her and Philip facing each other. She also struck groats in joint names and in hers alone, depicting only her profile bust. There were also halfgroats and pennies of similar style, but these are scarce finds.

The reign of the following monarch, Elizabeth I, saw many new innovations in the coinage. Gold sovereigns, crowns, angels and their fractions were produced, but also two new coins, the pound and half pound, of twenty and ten shillings respectively. Elizabeth's reign also saw the resumption of the silver crown and halfcrown, and the introduction of new fractions, the threepence, threehalfpence and threefarthings. These were distinguished by the presence of a rose behind the queen's head and a date on the reverse. Sometimes one finds a threehalfpence or threefarthings which has had the rose and date erased, in an attempt to pass them off as the slightly higher value halfgroat or penny. One of the most significant aspects as far as numismatic history is concerned is the advent of milled or machine made coins during the reign of Elizabeth, struck only between 1561 and 1571.

With the death of Elizabeth, the English throne passed to the king of Scotland, James VI, who as James I of England ceased to place the numeral VI on either his Scottish or English issues. His English gold coins continued some previous denominations, but also saw the advent of the twenty shilling unite, which in turn was replaced by the laurel. His silver issues comprised the crown, halfcrown, shilling, sixpence, halfgroat, penny and half-

penny. Also, for the first time in England, a regular copper coinage was provided, in the form of token farthings being struck under licence.

The monetary history of the reign of James's son and successor Charles I is very varied, and made all the more complex by the Civil War. Before his break with Parliament, Charles struck coins in London, and also at a mint in Aberystwyth, which utilised Welsh silver mines. The most commonly found coins of Charles tend to be lower denominations of the Tower of London mint, from the shilling down, struck during the period 1625-42, before the rift with Parliament. From 1643 until the king's execution in 1649, Parliament continued to strike coins at the Tower in Charles's name, but during this latter period a number of provincial mints also struck coins, including some very rare and crude coins produced in Royalist strongholds that were besieged by Parliamentarian troops. Also during Charles's reign, another short-lived attempt was made at machine production, and between 1631 and 1639 a series was produced under the aegis of Nicholas Briot, but these seldom occur as field finds. Charles also continued to license the production of copper farthings, and the final issue, the 'rose' farthing of 1636-44, was struck in great quantity.

During the period of the Commonwealth, a series of hammered gold and silver coins was struck, all bearing the same types and legends. Between 1656 and 1658 a series of milled coins bearing the name and portrait of Oliver Cromwell was produced. All are very rare and none to date appear to have been recovered in excavations or as a field find.

When Charles II was restored to the throne in 1660, for the first two years of his reign, a series of hammered gold and silver was produced. This was superseded by mechanisation In 1662, and thereafter all production was by means of coin presses. The old hammered coinage continued to circulate but was finally demonetised during the reign of William III.

Scotland

James V (1513-42) introduced several new and rarely-found gold denominations, a new style profile groat tariffed at one shilling and sixpence, and a one-third groat or sixpence. A debased sixpence and threepence, the bawbee and half bawbee, appeared in 1538.

The Scottish coinage underwent radical change during the reign of Queen Mary. A number of new gold denominations were introduced, along with a new silver testoon and half testoon, and a crown-sized silver ryal. Mary's base silver issues were added to with a three-halfpence coin known as a 'hardhead' and a penny, and during her marriage to the French dauphin Francis a twelvepenny groat called a 'nonsunt'. The coinage of James VI can be divided into two parts. Prior to his accession to the English Throne, he introduced new gold denominations, and a whole range of silver pieces such as silver ryals and their fractions and merks and their fractions. In 1578 the coinage was revalued, and coins of Mary still circulating were countermarked. Following his coronation as James I of England, his silver took on an English appearance, although tariffed differently. The Scottish sixty shillings was equivalent to the English crown of five shillings, and fractions *pro rata*. The latter part of James's reign saw a prolific coinage of copper twopences, or turners, and somewhat scarcer pennies.

The Scottish coinage under Charles I continued with issues of coins of similar style and equivalent weights but different tariffs from English issues. It was during Charles's reign that the use of the screw press supplanted the hammering method and in contrast to the situation in England, his son Charles II issued no hammered coinage.

As in the medieval period, certain foreign coins circulated in Britain, with gold coins being accepted according to their value by weight. Between 1554 and 1561 Spanish silver coins were legal tender, and some coins struck for use in Ireland seem to have seen a degree of circulation in Britain.

Site Finds

Coins of the Tudor and Stuart periods are more prolific as site finds than those of any other era, save that of the Roman period. This reflects the active economy of the age, with many new denominations coming into use, and a noticeable increase in higher denomination coins that occur as site finds.

Coin finds of Henry VII are usually halfgroats and sovereign pennies, with just the occasional full groat occurring. The same is true of Henry VIII, with base issue halfgroats (recalled under Elizabeth) also occurring as occasional finds, and seemingly far commoner than contemporary pennies or halfpennies. A small but growing body of the tiny farthings of Henry VIII is also being recorded, suggesting that their use may have been quite general, although their tiny size must mitigate against the recovery rate. Coins of Edward VI are scarce finds, although shillings, an unusually high denomination for casual loss, seem to be in evidence. Coin finds of Mary tend to be predominately groats, which turn up with some frequency, and sometimes show evidence of deliberate damage, or *'damnatio'*; this may be a consequence of her policy of religious persecution, but as this was not exclusive to Mary's reign it was perhaps Mary's marriage that was being damned. The commonest finds of Elizabeth are sixpences, threepences, halfgroats and pennies, with threehalfpences and threefarthings being less in evidence, and just the occasional shilling. Shillings and sixpences are more widespread under James I and Charles I, which suggest an increase in the use of higher denominations in the market place. Other finds of this period are commonly halfgroats and pence. During the Commonwealth, halfgroats and pennies constitute the bulk of field finds. The hammered coinage of Charles II is scarce, and is mainly confined to threepences, halfgroats and pennies. As with the medieval period, gold coins occur as single finds with sufficient frequency as to suggest that some individual coins may have changed hands, although their main use was probably that of wealth storage. An account of 1659 at Holkham Hall in Norfolk lists a property transaction in which money was "taken out of the closett and paid to Mr. Newgate in full his purchase money, £2,300." That was a massive sum for the time and one might presume that it was held in gold coin, few of which probably ever saw actual circulation.

The copper token farthings issued under James I and Charles I are frequent field finds. With the earlier types such as the 'Harrington', 'Lennox', 'Richmond' and 'Maltravers', distribution seems to have been sporadic, with field finds clustering in certain areas but not in others. A great number that circulated were forgeries, leading to their replacement with the 'rose' farthing. These latter are by far the commonest and many may simply have been discarded after their demonetisation.

As in medieval times, there were certain periods in which Scottish and English coins were used both sides of the border. In Scotland, English 'sovereign' pennies of Henry VII sometimes occur, and it is not uncommon to find Scottish coins south of the Border, perhaps associated with the great cattle droves of the time. Scottish finds from northern England include James VI hardheads, turners and placks and Charles I turners, all of which are also frequent finds in Scotland. Further south, Scottish copper rarely occurs, due perhaps to the proliferation of 'royal farthings' then being struck under licence. However, the silver twenty pence seems to have circulated quite widely in England, perhaps being used as a threehalfpenny denomination to supplement the English pennies and halfgroats, which are quite prolific.

Forgery was a common problem during Tudor and Stuart times, and false coin, often of plated base-metal, is found with some frequency. The regal token farthings of the early seventeenth century were forged on a widespread basis.

English Coins

Gold

Henry VIII (1509-47) angel

James I (1603-25) halfcrown © A. H. Baldwin

Charles I (1625-49) double crown © A. H. Baldwin

Charles I crown © CNG

Silver

Halfcrown

Charles I (1625-49)

Shillings

Edward VI (1547-53)

Elizabeth I (1558-1603)

James I (1603-25)

James I (1603-25)

Charles I (1625-49) © A. H. Baldwin

Charles I (1625-49)

Sixpences

Groats and fractions

Edward VI (1547-53)

Henry VII (1485-1509) profile bust groat

Philip and Mary (1554-8)

Henry VIII (1509-47) profile bust groat

51

Henry VIII facing bust groat

Henry VIII halfgroat, Canterbury

*Henry VIII (posthumous coinage) halfgroat,
Canterbury*

Philip & Mary (1554-8) groat

Elizabeth I (1558-1603) threepence

Elizabeth I halfgroat

James I (1603-25) halfgroat

Charles I (1625-49) halfgroat

Commonwealth (1649-60) halfgroat

Charles II (1660-85) threepence

Pennies and fractions

*Henry VIII (1509-47) 'sovereign-type' penny,
Durham*

Henry VIII halfpenny

Henry VIII farthing

Philip and Mary (1554-8) base penny

Elizabeth I (1558-1603) penny

Elizabeth I threefarthings

Elizabeth I halfpenny

James I (1603-25) portrait penny

Charles I (1625-49) 'rose' penny

Commonwealth (1649-60) penny

Copper-alloy regal token farthings

James I (1603-25) 'Harrington' type

James I 'Lennox' type

Charles I (1625-49) 'Richmond' type

Charles I 'Maltravers' type

Charles I 'rose' type

Scottish Coins

Gold

Mary (1542-67) twenty-two shillings © CNG

James VI (1567-25) sword and sceptre piece
© CNG

Silver and copper-alloy

James V (1513-42) Bawbee © CNG

Mary (1542-67) plack © M.R. Vosper

Mary penny © CNG

Francis & Mary (1558-60) lion

James VI (1567-1625) quarter thistle merk © CNG

James VI plack

James VI hardhead

James VI turner (pre-accession)

James VI turner (post-accession)

Charles I (1625-49) twenty pence

Charles I turner

Coins from overseas found in Britain, 16th and 17th Centuries *(silver unless otherwise indicated)*

Denmark

Christian III (1503-59) skilling

54

Frederic III (1609-70) two skillings

Charles I (1625-49) 'Ormonde money' groat

France

François I (1515-40) douzain

François I liard au dauphin

Henri II (1547-1559) douzain

Ireland

Elizabeth I (1558-1603) Æ penny © CNG

James I (1603-25) shilling

Italy

Venice, Leonardo Laurendon (1501-21) soldino

Venice, Antonio Priuli (1618-23) soldo

Latvia

Livonian Order, Herman von Bruggenei
(1535-49) schilling

Low Countries

Brabant, Charles V (1506-20) gros

Netherlands, Albert & Isabella (1598-1621)
patard

Netherlands, Albert & Isabella Æ liard

Netherlands, Overijssel 2 Stuivers 1619

*Liege, Maximillian Henri de Davière
(1650-88) Æ liard*

Friesland Æ duit 1675

Flanders, Charles II (1665-1700) Æ liard

Spain

Charles V & Joanna (1516-56) gold escudo

Louis XIII (1610-43) of France Æ seiseno 1642

*Felipe IV (1621-65) Æ eight maravedis
(with countermarks)*

Contemporary forgeries

*England: Elizabeth I copper-alloy 'sixpence',
originally silver-plated*

England: a crude copy of a regal token farthing

Scotland: Charles I turner

5
LATER COINS

Historical background

The reign of Charles II saw the return of religious conflict, and his successor, James II, was forced to flee to France after trying to re-establish the Catholic faith. William of Orange was offered the British thrones, which he took as King William II (Scotland) and III (England), ruling jointly for a time with his wife Mary, James's daughter.

During the reign of Queen Anne, England and Scotland were united by the Act of Union of 1707. The accession of George I, Elector of Hanover, in 1714 ushered in the era we now call the 'Georgian Period', but George barely had time to establish himself when his claim to the throne was challenged by the son of James II in 1715 (the Old Pretender). This threat was defeated, as was the subsequent invasion launched by James's grandson Charles (Bonnie Prince Charlie) in 1745, during the reign of George II.

Warfare continued to punctuate the eighteenth century, with France once again being the main adversary. Following the capture of Quebec, Britain dominated most of North America, whilst in India the British East India Company ran much of the sub-continent. Colonies were established in Australia and New Zealand, the Irish Act of Union was passed and the Empire continued to grow. The end of the eighteenth century saw the American War of Independence, and further conflict with France as Britain stood against the ambitions of Napoleon. This culminated in the battles of Trafalgar (1805) and Waterloo (1815).

Against all this military activity, Britain experienced much social change. Steam-powered textile mills, and the employment they offered, brought people flocking from the countryside to the new industrial towns. Social reformers campaigned against slavery and child labour, voting rights were extended, and scientists made many advances in medicine.

In literature, men such as Samuel Johnson, Robert Burns, Wordsworth, Coleridge, Keats and Shelley all left their mark.

The accession of Queen Victoria continued the progression towards modern ideas and values, although warfare was never far away, and the 1850s saw both war in the Crimea and the Indian Mutiny. British troops fought in Afghanistan, and involvement in Africa led to conflict with the Zulus and the Anglo-Boer wars.

The conflicts which had embroiled Britain reflected events on a wider stage, as other countries also vied for empire. The nineteenth century saw the unification of Germany and Italy, and the Empires of Russia and Turkey were at their zenith. Imperial tensions and ambitions reached breaking point in 1914, when Germany attacked France through Belgium and Britain, under treaty obligation to Belgium, declared war on Germany. The armistice of 1918 led to an uneasy peace that lasted for just twenty-one years, after which hostilities were resumed. Final peace in 1945 saw the political face of Europe change, with the establishment of the Eastern Bloc under the rule of Russia, itself finally collapsing in the closing years of the twentieth century.

For Britain, history has come full circle in many ways, with Scotland and Wales gaining greater independence, British troops returning to fight on old battlegrounds, and a re-emergence of superstition and fundamentalism in direct challenge to enlightenment and science.

The Coinage

As mentioned earlier, coin production using screw presses was undertaken on a number of occasions, but it was not until 1662 that hand-struck coins were finally abandoned in favour of machine production.

The new milled coinage instigated under Charles II consisted of gold pounds (known as 'guineas') in multiples of five, two, one and halves. Silver comprised crowns, half-crowns, shillings, sixpences, and four, three, two and one penny coins. Copper halfpennies and farthings were struck, as were tin farthings which contained a small plug of copper. Tin farthings were discontinued in 1692, but otherwise the pattern of coinage remained the same until the reign of George III.

In 1762, a new guinea fraction, the quarter guinea, was struck, to be followed by a seven shilling third-guinea in 1797. Also in 1797, to supplement the demand for copper coinage, a new issue of twopenny pieces and pennies was produced at the Soho mint in Birmingham. These new coins, manufactured on newly developed steam presses, were very unwieldy and unpopular, and on account of their size are known as 'cartwheel' coins. In 1799 they were replaced with smaller halfpennies and farthings, to be followed in 1806 by yet another issue of pennies, halfpennies and farthings. Also during this period silver coinage was supplemented with countermarked Spanish eight real coins and silver bank tokens. In 1816 a completely new coinage was introduced, in which the guinea was replaced by a gold five pound and two pound coin, and a one pound sovereign and it's half. Banknotes also came into more general use.

During the reign of Victoria the possibility of a decimal coinage was mooted, and a new two shilling silver coin, the florin, was introduced, followed by a short-lived issue of double florins. The copper coinage was supplemented by fractional farthings, intended for use overseas. In 1860 the copper coinage was replaced with a new bronze issue, which continued until decimalisation in the reign of Elizabeth II. A nickel-brass threepenny coin replaced the silver one in 1937. In 1920 the silver coinage was debased, and in 1947 was replaced entirely with cupro-nickel coins.

Decimal coinage was introduced in Britain in 1971, to be followed by a succession of new denominations and issues. The new coinage came to consist of cupro-nickel fifty, twenty, ten and fivepence coins, and copper twopennies, pennies and halfpennies. In 1983 a nickel-brass one pound coin was introduced, to be followed by a two pound coin in nickel-brass, and later in nickel-brass with a cupro-nickel inner. Since the introduction of the decimal coinage, there have been several adjustments to the size of the coins, and the halfpenny was discontinued. In addition a whole range of coins in gold, silver and base metals has been produced aimed at the collector and bullion markets, with very few actually seeing circulation.

In Scotland, during the reign of Charles II, the production of milled coins was commenced at the same time as in England, although the gold coinage was discontinued. Charles's coinage comprised a silver four merks tariffed at just over five English shillings, with two, one and half fractions, to be followed by a short-lived issue of silver dollars and fractions. A copper coinage of bawbees (sixpences) and turners or bodles was also produced, and these continued until 1697. James II instigated a coinage based on a silver sixty shillings, which with spasmodic fractions of forty, twenty, ten and five continued to be produced until the Act of Union.

As in proceeding periods, certain foreign coins also circulated, and forgery continued to be a problem.

Site Finds

Gold coins are scarce finds, but enough occur to demonstrate their part in the currency pool. Although no five or two guinea coins have been reported by metal detectorists, guineas and fractions of guineas do occur, and with greater frequency it would seem than later sovereigns, the circulatory use of which generally ceased in the early part of the twentieth century. Occasionally pierced gold coins are found, perhaps lost from watch chains.

High denomination silver coins are seldom found; few crowns are recorded, and even halfcrowns, often very worn, are not common until the mid-twentieth century. During the late seventeenth century silver bullion prices rose to such an extent that silver coins were worth more than their face value. This led to most silver coins being melted down or exported, a situation that continued intermittently throughout the eighteenth century. Consequently very few shillings or sixpences of this period circulated and were lost, although sixpences are occasionally found, predominantly those of William III, of which many have been bent into an 's' shape. It has been suggested that such coins were exchanged as 'love tokens', the numbers found perhaps being discards that suggest that the path of true love then, as now, did not always run true. The degree of wear on most suggests that this custom was probably at its most prevalent after the re-coinage of 1816, which rendered such issues obsolete. Shillings and sixpences of the new coinage, often in quite unworn condition, are not uncommon field finds. Occasional finds of Stuart period 'Maundy' type silver coins also illustrate their general monetary use. Nineteenth century silver fourpennies and threepennies are rarely unearthed.

Copper halfpennies and farthings dating from the late seventeenth to early nineteenth centuries are prolific finds, and copper and bronze small change continues until the present day. Particularly evident are farthings of Charles II and William III, and halfpennies of William III, George II and George III. Farthings of the two latter monarchs are scarcer. Tin farthings are surprisingly common, but often go unrecognised due to their susceptibility to corrosion. 'Cartwheel' pennies of George III are fairly common finds, unlike the corresponding two penny piece. In relative terms, fewer decimal coins seem to occur as field finds, due perhaps to the mechanised nature of modern farming coupled with the use of chemical rather than organic fertilisers, although they are prolific

on activity sites such as fairgrounds, parks and beaches, where they are lost in use or from pockets in clothing.

The types of foreign coins found reflect the extent of British colonial and military exploits during the past few centuries. But whilst some coins are undoubtedly simply souvenirs, others circulated alongside regal issues. Copper *duits* from the various provinces of the Netherlands and French *liards* were farthing-sized, and were used as such. French and Italian ten and five *centimes* and *centesimi* were of the same size and weight as British pennies and halfpennies and circulated widely. In order to drive them out of circulation, from 1887 they could be redeemed for stamps at the rate of thirteen centimes to the shilling. Quite significant numbers of coins current in Europe and the Middle East during the period of the two world wars seem to have found their way into the ground, having presumably been brought back by returning soldiers, to be lost or discarded. However, without this known historical background, such finds would be enigmatic - something to perhaps consider with earlier 'exotic' finds?

English and British Coins

Gold

Charles II (1660-85) guinea

George III (1760-1820) 'spade' guinea

George III one-third guinea

George III sovereign

Victoria (1837-1901) half sovereign

Silver *(unless otherwise indicated)*

Crown

Victoria (1837-1901) © A.H. Baldwin

Halfcrowns

James II (1685-88) © A.H. Baldwin

George III (1760-1820) new coinage

George VI (1936-52)

Florins

Victoria (1837-1901) 'old head' coinage

George V (1910-36)

Elizabeth II (Cu-Ni) (1952-)

Shillings

Anne (1702-14)

George I (1714-27) © A.H. Baldwin

George IV (1820-30)

George V (1910-36)

George VI (Cu-Ni) (1936-52)

Sixpences

William III (1694-1702)

George II (1727-60) © A.H. Baldwin

George III (1760-1820) new coinage

William IV (1830-7)

Victoria (1837-1901) 'young head' coinage

Edward VII (1901-10)

Elizabeth II (Cu-Ni) (1952-)

Fourpences

William and Mary (1688-94)

William IV (1830-7)

Threepences

Charles II (1660-85) milled issue

William III (1694-1702)

Twopences

William III (1694-1702)

George II (1727-60)

Pennies

William III (1694-1702)

Copper Alloys (unless otherwise indicated)

Threepennies

George VI (1936-52)

Elizabeth II (1952-)

Pennies

George III (1797 only) - the same design as the rarely-encountered larger twopence

George IV (1820-30)

Victoria (1837-1901) 'young head' coinage

Victoria 'old head' coinage

George V (1910-36)

Elizabeth II (1952-)

Halfpennies

William & Mary (1688-94)

William III (1694-1702)

George II (1727-60) © A.H. Baldwin

George III (1760-1820) first issue © A.H. Baldwin

George III third issue © A.H. Baldwin

George III fourth issue

William & Mary (1688-94) tin issue © Spink

Victoria (1837-1901) 'young head' coinage

George I (1714-27) 'dump' issue

Edward VII (1901-10)

George III (1760-1820) first issue

Elizabeth II (1952-)

George III third issue

Farthings

Charles II (1660-85)

George III fourth issue

George IV (1820-30)

Victoria (1837-1901) first issue

Victoria 'young head' second issue

Edward VII (1901-10)

George V (1910-36)

George VI (1936-52)

Decimal Coinage; Elizabeth II (1952-)
issued from 1971

Copper alloys and copper-clad iron-alloy

Two pounds

One pound

Fifty pence (old type)

Twenty pence

Ten pence (old type)

65

Five pence (old type)

Two pence

One penny

Halfpenny

Scottish Coins
Silver *(unless otherwise indicated)*

Charles II (1660 - 85) merk

Charles II sixteenth dollar

William and Mary (1689-94) Æ turner

William II (III) (1694-1702) Æ bawbee

Anne (1702-14) five shillings

Coins from overseas found in Britain
China

Kao Tsung (1736-95) Æ cash

France

Louis XV (1715-74) silver tenth-écu

Louis XVI (1774-93) Æ liard

Napoleon III (1852-70) Æ ten centimes

Æ five centimes 1914

Germany

Æ (Cu-Ni) ten pfennigs 1874

Æ one pfennig 1938

Zinc five pfennigs 1941

Guernsey

Victoria (1837-1901) Æ four doubles

Ireland

James II (1685-91) Æ 'gun money' shilling -
there are similar coins in many denominations

George II (1727-60) Æ halfpenny

George III (1760-1820) Æ halfpenny © M.R. Vosper

Nickel Sixpence 1940

Isle of Man

Victoria (1837-1901) Æ farthing

Italy

Victor Emmanuel II (1837-1901)
Æ five centesimi

Jersey

George VI (1936-52) Æ twelfth shilling

Elizabeth II (1952-) Æ decimal penny

Netherlands

West Friesland Æ duit 1739

Gelderland Æ duit 1766

Holland Æ duit 1766

Overijssel Æ duit 1767

Portugal

John V (1706-50) gold quartinho

Russia

Peter the Great (1682-1725) Æ kopek

Nicholas I (1825-55) Æ kopek

Sweden

Charles XII (1697-1718) Æ sixth öre

Turkey

Abdul Hamis II (1876-1909) silver two kurush

Contemporary forgeries

British George III struck silver-gilt 'sovereign'

British George III struck 'halfpenny'

British Elizabeth II cast 'pound'

6
TOKENS, JETONS AND MEDALS

In addition to currency coins struck by rulers and governments, there is a large body of numismatic material that falls into other categories.

Tokens

Tokens in the numismatic sense are coins that represent a notional rather than an intrinsic value, and were usually intended to be redeemed for coins of the realm. They might be exchanged just as one exchanges coins for goods or services, or they may be given in return for a certain amount of labour, such as hop or pea picking, to be redeemed later. Tokens date back to Roman times, and there is a famous series depicting erotic scenes. These, it has been speculated, may have been entrance tickets to brothels, or were redeemable for different services at various tariffs.

Tokens were often issued during periods of currency shortage. The regally sanctioned token farthings already mentioned ceased to be produced after 1644, and this hiatus was filled by local traders taking it upon themselves to issue a copper token coinage. Between 1648 and 1672, a wide range of entrepreneurs began striking their own tokens. These were mostly farthings and halfpennies, but some pennies were also struck. The tokens were produced using screw presses, and were probably manufactured in London and possibly other regional centres to the order of the traders as required. Such tokens are relatively common field finds, with new examples being recorded from time to time. Another major period of token production occurred in the eighteenth century, when the copper currency, spasmodic and forgery-ridden, was supplemented by tokens, predominately halfpennies. These issues comprise tokens produced by traders who are named upon them, and also tokens made anonymously for general circulation. The

popularity of these new tokens led to some being struck for advertising purposes and it became a popular pastime to form collections of them, which in turn led to others being produced purely for collectors. Forgeries of eighteenth century tokens are common, as their production carried the same profit potential as forging regal coins, but without the same degree of criminal risk. For this reason another type of token was produced known as an 'evasion'. These had fictitious legends and bore only a superficial resemblance to regal coins, but were sufficiently similar in appearance to allow them to be passed off as legal tender to the unwary.

As well as the early nineteenth century silver bank tokens mentioned in the last chapter, private silver tokens were also produced between 1811-12, and from around 1811 to 1815, another series of private copper tokens was struck. These were predominately pennies, some of 'cartwheel' size, as well as some halfpennies and farthings. Another type of token at this time involved the recycling of worn (and often forged) George II and George III regal halfpence, by stamping them with the name of a trader who would redeem them. However, a growing trend amongst unscrupulous traders in not redeeming tokens led to their prohibition by an act of Parliament in 1817.

Copper was not the only medium used for tokens, and lead proved to be very popular, as it required very little investment of technology to produce them. Many were simply cast in open moulds. Lead tokens are widespread, and can be dated from the medieval period through to the nineteenth century. A sixteenth century account states that lead tokens were used in London in lieu of pennies, halfpennies and farthings, but others may have been used as checks or tallies, as with the hop tokens widely used in Kent. A wide range of designs have been noted ranging from heraldic motifs to unintelligible patterns. Many simply carry initials. An interesting series was produced in East Anglia, centred on Bury St Edmunds but also produced at other locations, and relates to a custom in which a choir boy was chosen to act as bishop on the feast of St Nicholas, the patron saint of children. The boy would be given tokens which he would distribute amongst poor children which they could use to buy food.

Other classes of token in use until recently include market tallies, tool checks and shop checks, mostly struck in copper-alloys.

Jetons

Jetons are coin-like pieces, originally used for calculating sums, and were first introduced in the thirteenth century. Before the introduction of Arabic numerals, calculation could not be done using arithmetic. The means employed were abaci, upon which rows of beads were slid, or chequer boards or cloths, upon which counters were moved. Prior to the production of jetons specifically intended for calculation, other types of counter, including possibly actual coins, were used.

In the Middle Ages, the main centre for the production for jetons was France, although they were also produced in England in the thirteenth and early fourteenth centuries, the dies sometimes employing the same punches used on the coins of the time. In the sixteenth century Nürnberg in Germany also came to the fore as a centre of jeton production, and German jetons were imported into Britain in vast quantities during the sixteenth and seventeenth centuries, with the 'rose/orb' type predominating. These were issued by a number of successive guild masters, the early ones being anonymous. Manual calculating finally gave way to arithmetic at the end of the seventeenth century, although jetons continued to be produced as presentation pieces and gaming counters right up until the early twentieth century.

Medals

Medals may be defined as presentation or commemorative pieces, and as such date to at least Roman times, although the boundary between coin and medal can sometimes be rather blurred. During the European Renaissance the casting or striking of highly artistic medals became popular, and commemoratives made their appearance in Britain during the Tudor period. Their use as military awards dates from the seventeenth century although they were not issued as general campaign and service medals until the nineteenth century. Commemorative medals with a patriotic theme were popular during the nineteenth and twentieth centuries, many being struck in base metal and given out by local authorities or schools to celebrate coronations and royal jubilees. Today there is an active production of souvenir medals sold at tourist outlets, as well as art medals and commemorative and presentation pieces.

Site Finds

Lead tokens from all periods occur as field finds, although certain locations can produce larger concentrations, presumably reflecting some specific local use. Some lead tokens have been found cut in half, suggesting their use as monetary fractions. Copper-alloy medieval jetons are also common, and on occasion seem to appear more frequently in fields near to locations with monastic connections. Nürnberg jetons of the sixteenth and seventeenth centuries are very common finds, and there is some suggestion that these were also used as a substitute for small change, although that cannot be proven. But given that they seem to proliferate at a time when the use of the checker-board was declining, yet declined themselves around the time copper token farthings appeared, there is certainly a good argument for thinking that they had a token currency use. However they were used, the large number found reflects the economic vitality of the period.

Seventeenth century traders tokens occur in the same contexts as other coins of the period, either being lost in use or perhaps discarded when no longer redeemable. The accurate plotting and recording of tokens is invaluable in understanding their use, and confirming the locations of issuers. Eighteenth century tokens occur far less frequently, and official or forged regal coppers predominate with finds from this period. Nineteenth century silver and copper tokens were less widespread, and seem to be very rarely excavated.

Medals are occasionally found, and tend to be either base metal commemoratives, or twentieth century campaign medals. Some medals bear the name of the recipient, and it is sometimes possible to trace relatives and return them.

Lead-alloy tokens, counters and/or checks

Pictorial type (c.13th-15th centuries)

Geometric type (c.13th-15th centuries)

Irregular geometric type (c.13th-15th centuries)

Crowned rose/eagle (c.1554-8)

'Boy Bishop' type (16th century)

Lines and pellets (c.16th-18th centuries)

Pictorial type (c.16th-18th centuries)

Sexfoil/initials (c.17th-18th century)

Hop token (19th century, George Hood, Hawkhurst)

Copper-alloy tokens, counters and checks

17th century halfpenny, Essex, Rochford

17th century farthing, Gloucestershire, Bristol

17th century farthing, Suffolk, Clare

17th century octagonal halfpenny, Kent, Canterbury. Square and heart-shaped tokens are also known © M.R. Vosper

18th century halfpenny, Essex, Chelmsford

18th century 'evasion'

19th century penny, Birmingham workhouse

Shop dividend check

Public House check

George III 'spade guinea' counter

Political 'To Hanover' counter

Market check

Gaming machine token

English and French jetons

English, facing bust (c.1280-1345)

French, dolphin/cross (c.1365-1410)

English, triangle/cross (c.1307-27)

French, crown/cross (c.1385-1440)

French and English, king under canopy (c.1325-1400)

French, three lis/cross (c.1461-97)

English, heraldic (c.1345-1400)

French, châtel tournois/cross (c.1461-97)

French, shield/cross (c.1350-1500)

French, IHS/cross (c.1497-1521)

Low Countries and Nürnberg jetons

Nürnberg, French shield (c.1480-1500)

Low Countries, 'Venus' type (c.1490-1550)

Nürnberg, ship/lozenge (c.1490-1550)

Nürnberg, Lion of St Mark/lis (c.1500-1570)

Nürnberg, rose/orb type (c.1500-1635) - there are several issuers, anonymous and also named on the jetons.

Nürnberg, French-style, Hans Krauwinckel II (1586-1635)

Nürnberg, 'Turks head' type (c.1608-12)

Nürnberg, French style (c.1758-97)

Medals and medalets

Charles I commemorative medalet (17th century)

Religious medalet (17th century)

Victorian commemorative

British War Medal (1914-20)

Edwardian commemorative

Victory Medal (1914-18)

1914-15 Star

103212.
GNR. W. DAINES,
R. F. A.

Defence Medal (1939-45)

British War Medal (1939-45)

Campaign medal, Italy Star (1939-45)

6
MECHANISMS OF COIN LOSS

Hoards

The most spectacular type of coin find is that of the hoard, which can number from just a few coins to many thousands. Hoards occur from all periods of history, and most recently-found ones have been extensively studied and published.

The reasons for hoarding can be varied, but the usual assumption is that coins and other precious objects were buried for safe keeping, with the intention of recovering them at a future date, and that 'epidemics' of hoarding represent times of trouble. Evidence for this can be seen with quite recent history in eastern Germany. As the Russians advanced westwards at the close of World War Two, German civilians fled further west to the American and British lines. Some were killed, and their hoards have either been discovered since, or remain buried, but since the reunification of Germany, some elderly former refugees have been able to return and recover their valuables. Many hoards from the time of the British Civil War have also been found, but often from the areas of recruitment rather than of conflict, indicating soldiers who did not return. A well-documented example of hoarding in an emergency is that of Samuel Pepys, who buried a quantity of coins in 1667, when London was threatened by the Dutch Fleet.

But as well as hoarding during periods of crises, the practice must have been commonplace at other times as well. Banks are a fairly recent innovation, and in earlier times concealment was the only option to protect valuables from theft. Although hoards of ancient coins are generally found in the ground, not all were buried, and concealment within buildings was probably the more usual method. Excavations at the Roman town of Caistor in Norfolk revealed no fewer than twelve different hoards of coins, found within the ruins of collapsed buildings. But whether concealed within buildings or buried, most hoards were no doubt successfully retrieved, leaving no trace in the historical record. When a Roman 'villa' at Gestingthorpe in Essex was excavated, several ceramic pots of third or fourth century date were found in a position that suggested that they had originally been buried below the floor. They were empty, but had lids *in situ* - had they been used for coin storage? When hoards are found, they represent a failure, with the depositor either dying, or even forgetting the place of deposition, which was something that Pepys nearly did. Even 'epidemics' of hoarding need not represent emergencies; if there is a certain percentage of savings hoards that are not recovered through either death or forgetfulness, then 'epidemics' may only be a reflection of a proliferation of coinage at a particular period. And this need not represent a period of prosperity either - it may reflect inflation, with more coins needed to purchase the same amount of goods or services.

Another explanation for hoarding is one that modern minds sometimes have difficulty accepting, and that is votive deposit. It is increasingly clear that during periods such as the Bronze Age and Iron Age, artefacts were deliberately deposited as offerings to the gods. This could take the form of assemblages of artefacts such as those found at Flag Fen in Lincolnshire. Such offerings are often associated with watery environments (just as we still throw coins into fountains!), but also occur on dry land, for example in the precincts of temples. A wide-open arable field of today might well have contained a sacred grove in ancient times. A significant epidemic of hoarding took place in the late Bronze Age, with numerous deposits of tools and weapons, usually broken up, occurring. These are traditionally taken to be hoards buried for recovery by bronze smiths, who found that with the advent of iron their bronze had lost its value, and so the deposits were simply abandoned. Bronze however continued to be used for many other purposes after the advent of iron tools and weapons, and so a votive reason for burial seems equally possible, particularly when evidence has been found for some degree of curation of Bronze Age artefacts well into the Iron Age. In Denmark, votive hoards of weapons have been found that date not just from the Bronze Age, but also from the Viking period, with the weapons of defeated armies being broken up and thrown into bogs. The wealth placed in graves such as at Sutton Hoo is another manifestation of abandonment, and even the lavishing of huge sums of money by medieval magnates on churches in the name of God may be seen as a form of material sacrifice. There can be little doubt that assemblages of coins such as those recovered from Coventina's Well on Hardrian's Wall, or from the hot springs at Bath, represent individual coins, or maybe handfuls of coins, thrown in as votive offerings. It follows that burying complete hoards of coins in sacred places for religious reasons rather than for safety may have been commonplace.

Until the Treasure Act was passed in 1996, the old laws of Treasure Trove placed ownership of a find with the landowner if it seemed probable that the find had been lost or abandoned and not buried with the intent of recovery. The reasons for this seemingly strange criterion relate to the medieval origins of Treasure Trove, but the ruling placed a certain inhibition on history professionals who did not want to see academically significant finds being dispersed. Now that the law has changed, so too has the number of historians willing to openly consider hoards as being votive. This has been suggested for the Snettisham Iron Age groups, and even for the spectacular Hoxne hoard, and although this latter example is less convincing, it does add a further possible explanation for the reason behind the burial of some coin hoards.

Single Finds

When considering single coin finds as opposed to hoards, it is remarkable that so many individual coins found their way into the ground, and it seems unlikely that casual loss at the place of discovery can account for all of the coins found. It is probable that there were several different mechanisms at work, and these may well have varied at different times, depending on prevailing social and economic factors. Hoarding may still be an explanation for certain single coin finds, for if one might conceal a group of coins for either safety or votive purposes, it follows that the same might apply to high value single coins. Thus any high-status single find has to be considered in that context, or even as a single stray from a larger previously recovered group. Returning once more to Pepys, in his account he tells us that of the gold pieces that he had buried, some two dozen or so were unaccounted for on recovery, so if any still survive in the ground and were to be found now, they would give a completely false picture of the original deposit.

Votive deposition may also be an explanation for some single finds. The same motivation as mentioned above in respect of hoards may just as easily apply to individual coins. Perhaps Iron Age or Roman farmers routinely buried coins in a corner of their fields to encourage a good harvest, or even scattered a handful of coins onto the soil. Certainly evidence for votive deposition has been found on a number of sites. Temples are one kind of structure where individual coins and brooches have been found simply buried in the precinct, and in France, archaeologists have found Iron Age coins placed in the post holes of now-vanished buildings.

The apparent votive use of coins highlights a dichotomy in as far as coin use and loss is concerned in the Roman period in Britain. Early Roman coins, even low denominations such as *semisses* and *quadrantes*, common elsewhere in the Roman Empire of the time, are scarce site finds in

Britain. However, early coins outnumber later ones in votive deposits, as previously mentioned. This clearly demonstrates that early Roman coinage was reaching Britain, but was not being traded in the market place in a way as to make it easily lost. Early medieval coins are much rarer site finds than Iron Age or Roman ones, although some areas do have concentrations. A number of rural locations have been identified as 'productive sites' with speculation that they may have been open markets, rather like a present-day 'boot fair'. It is certainly true that the sites of modern fairgrounds and 'boot fairs' produce copious scatters of lost coins. However, few 'productive sites' have been subjected to any serious archaeological investigation, and agricultural distribution remains a plausible explanation, perhaps comprising imported waste from urban rather than rural sources. Occupation however might seem equally plausible, and when one 'productive site' was investigated archaeologically, considerable occupational evidence was found in the vicinity, and thus the finds may represent on-site losses comparable to sites of other periods and reflecting coin use at the time. In further pursuit of an alternative to the 'medieval boot fair' theory, it is worth mentioning that the seventh and eighth centuries were largely aceramic, and apart from coins, there were very few diagnostic metal small finds around to be lost, making coins stand out. Some 'productive sites' also produce strap-ends of the ninth century, suggesting continuing material deposition at a later time when coin use had become much rarer and another artefact type predominated. If more early medieval 'productive sites' are ever archaeologically excavated, it may be found that they reflect the same kind of occupational and land use activity prevalent with Roman and later medieval 'productive sites', which of course may well have included trading, but not exclusively so.

To the historian, coins, particularly ancient ones, are an invaluable source of information because they are often accurately dateable. Even when (as with most early examples) no actual date appears on the coin, other factors often allow them to be attributed quite closely. The fact that coins are dateable does not of course mean that they date associated finds. If a coin is found in an excavation along with a brooch, it may be that either the coin or the brooch was already old when lost. If coins of a certain date commonly occur in field scatters together with other artefacts of a particular type, it does not date the artefacts – there could have been different loss periods for each respective type of object. But when associations occur repeatedly, then probability does begin to link coins to other artefacts, and thus accurate coin identity and dating becomes important. When assessing the date of a coin's deposition, the degree of wear it exhibits must be taken into account. At the time of decimalisation in Britain, a considerable number of very worn Victorian bronze coins were still circulating, thus giving a possible loss date of up to a century after the coin was struck. It may be that ancient coins were used less frequently, and thus the amount of wear might indicate an even longer period of currency than a modern coin. In certain cases hoard evidence is useful in estimating wear rates, by comparing the earliest coins with the latest ones, although many hoards were selective and do not always reflect the typical coinage in everyday use.

Coins are very easy to miss in the course of archaeological excavation, and in consequence the coin lists for many sites are extremely sparse when compared to metal detected assemblages from arable land. Even when metal detectors are employed in excavations, their use is often limited to scanning stripped areas and thus they only tend to locate coins in buried features such as pits and ditches. Significant numbers of coins, unstratified and in the topsoil, will often be removed and dumped on spoil heaps, where only a tiny percent will remain within the range of metal detectors, should they even be employed. Archaeologists usually concern themselves with buried features, and small finds such as coins are incidental to the whole process. This means that significant diagnostic assemblages may simply be discarded, and so conventional archaeological excavation is often a poor source of information in trying to understand coin use and loss.

Metal detecting is probably the best method of establishing a coin use/loss pattern for any given area, but it is rarely carried out in an organised and consistent manner. Most hobby metal detectorists seek out productive areas and then concentrate on them, with relatively few accurately plotting and recording their finds. Although this situation is slowly improving, a lot of hobby metal detecting remains primarily trophy hunting, with finds rather than data being the main objective of most searchers. In order to produce a meaningful survey of a given area, it would be necessary to search, using GPS, in a measured grid pattern, covering non-productive as well as productive ground, being consistent in search speed and noting the actual time spent in searching. It would also be desirable to repeat the whole process a number of times over several cultivation cycles. Such a survey would clearly be very labour intensive, and in consequence few amateurs are likely to be inspired to do this. It is clear that in many cases, concentrations of coins accompanied by ceramics and other artefacts do represent sites *per se*, but by concentrating on an area, it has been demonstrated by excavation that such accumulations can build up through secondary deposition, with no evidence of any archaeology below. It is possible to illustrate the process of secondary deposition with the experience of one metal detectorist searching a large mixed arable farm. He repeatedly detected empty tubes of veterinary ointment on ploughed fields that had never been utilised for animal grazing. Such tubes were used within the confines of the farm itself, in the cowsheds. There they would be discarded, becoming incorporated into the waste that would be periodically spread onto the arable land as fertiliser. Given that such tubes were

only used for a few decades, and that he was finding on average one every few square metres, it demonstrates how just one type of secondary deposit, over a short period of time, can become a feature of surface collection. Multiply the range of items lost or discarded and the time scale of deposition, and it is clear that one must remain circumspect when evaluating the meaning of surface collection using metal detectors.

It is evident that many modern coins are lost where they are used. Many coins can be spotted on the ground in shopping centres and high streets, or near ticket machines and parking meters. A metal detector search of a fairground the day after the fair has gone will produce a good harvest of change lying in the grass, and searching parks and commons will produce a considerable scatter of buried coins. Some of these occur in small stacks, which suggests that they slid out of the trouser pocket of someone sitting on the grass. But what of earlier losses?

In trying to assess possible mechanisms of coin use and loss in past times, a number of variables need to be considered, and in many cases we simply do not have sufficient knowledge of prevailing circumstances to fully address them. The modern examples just mentioned require change to be carried on the person in a fairly casual way for loss to occur, which means that clothing fashion has to be factored in. In a portrait painting of a gentleman *c.*1770 by Joseph Wright, now in the National Gallery (NG6496), a circular object, presumed to be a coin, can be seen in the breeches pocket of the subject, so the potential for casual loss is still there, but the tightness of the garment probably makes it less likely to occur than with twentieth century trousers. And is it reasonable to suppose that Iron Age people also carried gold staters around in trouser pockets, or that Romano-Britons used loose change in a purchasing context on remote rural farms?

Gold coins, because of their high intrinsic value, have probably always been used in a different way to silver and base metal coins.

As mentioned previously, single finds of Roman gold coins are scarce in Britain, although they are more common in certain parts of Europe, where many are sufficiently worn as to suggest that they circulated there as part of a market economy. Neronian *aurei* frequently have more wear than later Roman gold, which proves that they were still accepted even after the demise of that hated emperor, but rarely enough wear to suggest that they circulated for many decades, unlike *denarii*. Later Roman gold is rarely worn to any degree, suggesting most coins were used as stored wealth, and some single finds were probably deliberate concealments rather than casual losses. Where gold coins are found in excavations, it might be possible to determine if they were lost or deposited by considering their context. It is clear from paintings and writings that gold coins were used in transactions in the later medieval and modern eras, but often such transactions may have been in parcels that were never passed from hand to hand like small change. Some gold coins such as seventeenth and eighteenth century guineas often exhibit considerable wear and clearly were handled frequently, but only by one stratum of society and perhaps reflecting a transient aspect of the economy at a particular time - one thinks of the coffee house culture and gambling rakes. In the memoirs of William Lawrence, a sergeant in Wellington's army, he gives an account of acquiring a third-guinea, or 'seven shilling piece' as he refers to it. The first thing he did was to change it in order to obtain spending money, its value being too great for most transactions.

A demonstration of gold coin use in Victorian times was provided by my grandfather, who recounted how his father had a number of sovereigns set aside to pay for his funeral and gravestone. In an era when few people had bank accounts, that was the only way to store wealth, and clearly these coins did not circulate for the whole time that they were stored. Contrast this to the Victorian 'bun' pennies and halfpennies still circulating in the 1960s. These showed that a coin could be worn smooth in a century, but this cannot be applied to all denominations at all times. In attempting to deduce coin use from wear, many variables have to be considered.

With silver and base-metal coins, loss from use is clearly a major mechanism in their deposition, but sometimes this is not a satisfactory explanation. One anomaly is that silver coinage of the eighteenth century rarely occurs as site finds, and is perhaps even scarcer than gold, yet mint statistics show that shillings and sixpences were minted in tens of thousands. Metal detecting however has demonstrated by negative evidence that few circulated to be lost, and this confirms contemporary accounts that tell us most silver coins were hoarded as soon as they were issued.

The sheer volume of late Roman base metal coins on some sites cannot be explained by everyday use and loss – it is difficult to see what use there would be for coin transactions on a rural farmstead unless they took it in turns to hold 'farmers markets'. Some modern coin loss can be demonstrated to occur through coins falling from pockets, but to our knowledge pockets were not a feature of ancient costume and thus other mechanisms for loss must be sought. Many base metal coins may simply have been discarded after having been demonetised in one of the frequent re-coinages, which the lack of wear on some oft-found types supports, whilst others may have been deliberately deposited as offerings as already suggested. Another possible explanation is that Roman rural sites, including 'villas', were not just the homesteads of extended families as has often been assumed, but may in fact have been nucleated settlements no different to the villages of the later Middle Ages, populated by many different families including butchers, bakers and candlestick makers who sold their goods to other villagers in exactly the same way as in modern villages. There may have been a regular procession of traders doing their rounds, and it may well be that by the third century there was as active a market economy in the countryside as in the towns. An indication that there might have been widespread on-site trading is evidenced by the large numbers of lead weights from Roman rural sites that are found. In attempting to interpret the population of the Roman countryside, surprisingly little archaeological excavation has been done, with most investigations being limited to parts of sites, not whole areas. Another factor in Roman coin loss may be that in the third and fourth centuries the only coins generally available were bronze radiates and *nummi*, with a disparity between them and the next readily obtainable higher denomination being possibly as great as that between the modern penny and a ten pound note. Their low value, together with obsolescence caused by frequent recoinages, may have made their loss or discarding of little significance. It is therefore perhaps not surprising that small late Roman bronzes are so prolific, whatever the cause of their deposition.

That coin loss can be related to locale is evidenced by seventeenth century tokens occurring in numbers around their place of issue. These may have been lost or possibly discarded after demonetisation, but their local origin is undeniable, although not always confined to the parish of origin. One particular farm in a parish that did not issue tokens has produced many from a neighbouring parish that did. Does this imply their currency in the parish of loss, or perhaps their importation with manure? And what of medieval gold coins that occur in remote rural areas? These are unlikely to have been votive deposits, and less likely to have been on-site casual losses. Is it not possible, indeed perhaps even likely, that many medieval coin losses could derive from the transportation of urban waste to the countryside for manuring purposes? It is quite possible that small rural communities would not produce enough organic waste and might look to obtaining more from urban areas, where it would be surplus to requirements and in fact a noisome liability. An account of 1794 concerning the agriculture of Essex stated that the Ilford area of that county was noted for its annual potato crop, only facilitated by what was described as liberal quantities of 'town manure'. This was most probably brought in from London, and it is a documented fact that in the nineteenth century a two-way coastal trade existed between Essex and London, with barges taking hay from the land to the horse-dependant city, and bringing back manure for use on the land. Might not a similar arrangement have existed in earlier times between town and country elsewhere? If this were the case it would explain how high status finds such as gold coins occur singly in what appear to be remote and impoverished areas. There remains considerable scope for further work into the mechanisms of coin use and loss, and many things that we may never know, but the more data that are recorded and published, the nearer we will come to answering some of these many puzzles.

7
THE SPATIAL DISPERSAL OF COINS

Agriculture has long been a prime factor in the discovery of coins and coin hoards, and the advent of metal detectors has greatly increased the number of such occurrences on arable land. When hoards are found *in situ* their composition is not in question, but frequently hoards are found which have been brought to the surface by ploughing, and thus the original integrity of the find is compromised. In such instances diligent searching of the surrounding area might be expected to recover most if not all of the original deposit, and subsequent publication would be an accurate reflection of the hoard. However, if in many cases substantial percentages of coins remain unrecovered, it would have implications for the interpretation of all plough-scattered hoards. In order to establish if there were parameters of probability that could be applied to this question, I decided to bury a control hoard, subject it to modern agricultural processes for a number of years, and then attempt to recover it using metal detectors.

This experiment was prompted by my own observations of metal detector use on a substantial Romano-British site in Suffolk during the 1980s. It was noticed that within a five hectare spread of Roman coins of mainly third and fourth century date, a number of Constantinian *nummi* with a distinctive patina were emerging, but were spread over an area of at least eighty metres. Additionally, occasional denarii were being found that also seemed to represent a discrete group, but again were spread at least fifty metres apart. The consequence of this was that against a 'background noise' of numerous other coins, neither group was recognised as a hoard by the finders, and the coins were dispersed.

Traditional archaeological fieldwalking techniques have always assumed that field surface finds can be plotted on the premise that their original deposition was in close proximity to their place of recovery. Although soil creep down slopes may on occasion be taken into account, for the most part it would seem that finds do not move greatly, and this has been confirmed by excavation of areas lying below scatters of finds.

The way in which agricultural activity affects ploughzone archaeology has been considered on a number of occasions in the past, and experiments have been conducted by monitoring the movements of lithic and ceramic samples. It would seem from such studies that the movement of different artefact classes such as flint flakes, cores and pebbles may not be consistent (Clark and Schofield, p.100 in Schofield, 1991). As all such sampling experiments have so far been confined to surface collection, and as coins may represent a further class with different movement characteristics, little can be deduced from models so far produced as they would have to be modified to consider the three-dimensional sampling methodology outlined here.

The test hoard was buried in 1985, with recovery commencing in 2001. The coins chosen were one hundred decimal pennies, which at that time were unclad copper-alloy and approximated in metal detector response to high status hoard coins such as aurei, denarii and sterling pennies etc. The location selected was a flat arable field of no known archaeological significance; a preliminary search of the ploughsoil by fieldwalking and metal detecting failed to reveal any evidence of archaeology or a significant amount of metallic small finds. The depth of burial selected was twenty-five centimetres. This is below most pre-twentieth century cultivation levels, but at the limit of most present-day procedures, the intention being to simulate a hoard brought into the cultivation zone in modern times. The coins were placed loose into a flat bottomed hole. Each coin was countermarked to prevent contamination by chance loss of an unrelated coin.

During the following twelve years, the field was subjected to annual arable use, the crops being cereals with rape and beans used as break crops. Cultivation was by means of six and eight-furrow reversible mouldboard ploughs, power harrows and rollers, with sub-soiling being carried out on several occasions using a twin tine chisel plough and a mole plough on one occasion. Ploughing depth varied between 20-25cm, the chisel plough to around 45cm and the mole plough at about 60cm. The power harrows operated at around 15cm. Cultivation was in alternate directions each year.

The hoard was left for five years, and then checked in 1990 using a metal detector. Coins found were excavated and plotted, and then reburied exactly as found. A group of eighty-three coins remained at the point of deposition, three more lay in a line at 1m intervals and at a 30° angle from the direction of cultivation. Three more were located further south in a fairly direct line, the furthest being 20m away. Thus eighty-nine coins were recoverable within five years of the first cultivation.

After sixteen years it was decided to attempt the total recovery of the hoard. The metal detectors chosen were both 'top of the range' units, and would represent the best that hobby metal detectorists would be likely to employ. One was able to give a diagnostic signal response on a test penny buried flat at 15cm, the other unit gave a diagnostic response on the same target at a maximum of 22cm. Coins buried on edge produced a much reduced response depending on angle of search coil pass, varying at between 10-15cm.

The first search was carried out in the Spring of 2001, on a rolled seedbed, over an initial target area of 10m². No response was received at the point of the original hoard burial, but twenty-one coins were recovered within a 5m radius, all single finds but for two which were lying together. A wider search pattern produced two further coins. Another search was carried out in the Autumn of 2001 which produced a further twenty-two coins. A wider search pattern and random prospecting further out produced no result. Searching resumed in April 2003, again on a rolled seedbed. On consecutive visits the finds totals were seven, three and five. Searching was extended beyond the immediate area and along the lines of cultivation for 80m in all directions with no result. A final visit was made in December 2003 following a further cultivation phase, with the field again a flat rolled seedbed. A 20m radius of the original square was searched and three further coins were recovered. This gave a total of sixty-three coins recovered, thirty-seven still unaccounted for.

The failure to recover 37% of a hoard buried in known circumstances and searched for methodically and repeatedly clearly does have implications in assessing other agriculturally dispersed hoards. It is known from the accounts of some hoard finders that they have assumed total recovery after only a few subsequent visits, so clearly there is much scope for reappraisal. The first thing to consider is the displacement of coins by agricultural equipment – what evidence is there for significant movement? A reversible plough inverts soil, but causes little lateral movement. Sub-soilers are unlikely to cause significant lateral movement and will not come into contact with all but a tiny proportion of buried material; however if a tine or mole went directly though a buried body of coins it could theoretically have a significant dispersal effect within a limited area. The greatest amount of dispersal seems to occur with the use of secondary cultivators (Clark and Schofield, p.100). A further permutation might apply to hoards buried near to the edge (headland) of a field. Large reversible ploughs may be withdrawn at some distance from the headland, and if withdrawn at the location of a hoard could result in considerable displacement of buried coins. Additionally, once a plough has been withdrawn, reversed and re-inserted, any small find adhering to a ploughshare will then travel down the field to the opposite end, and be re-inserted for the next pass, thus providing the opportunity for a find to be dislodged at any point down this 180° axis. On one occasion two parts of one artefact (a Victorian brooch) were found at opposite ends of a fifteen hectare field – perhaps such mechanisms at work?

There are, however, other factors which might be considered and which may have a quite drastic displacement effect. One is the movement of small finds on the wheels of tractors. In conversation with a farm worker it was described to me how Roman coins had been found on a farmyard hardstanding after mud had been pressure-hosed from a tractor's wheels, the probable site of origin being a half mile drive along a metalled road! Other ways in which coins could be relocated is through the dumping of soil washed from sugar beet grown in a different field, or the infilling of hollows or small gravel pits with soil from elsewhere.

But what is perhaps striking about the displacement of the test hoard is that none of the coins in this case were recovered outside a 20m radius of the original place of deposition. If any have migrated further they were not located, although it was not possible to grid the entire field with close accuracy. The balance of probability, however, suggests that most of the thirty-seven missing coins remain within the 20m radius, but have not been detected. It was noticed that many coins found subsequent to the initial searches were within the grid area that had already been searched, indicating how much margin there is for error even when searching meticulously. Even though one of the metal detectors used could theoretically detect a single coin at the maximum cultivation depth, this would not apply if coins were now buried on edge. It would presumably take many ploughings and consequently soil inversions to eventually present all missing coins flat and within range.

During the time this experiment was run-ning the question of hoard recovery became very relevant to me, as in 1992 I myself began finding late Roman gold *solidi* in a ploughed field in a neighbouring parish. These coins were recovered over a period of more than ten years regular searching with the aid of a metal detector, and were dispersed across an area of almost 100m. This seemed a quite remarkable spread always assuming that the coins were at one time a discrete group, which on the basis of similar finds seems probable, but in the light of the experiment described above perhaps not so remarkable if they had been in the plough-zone for a much longer period. On a site in Bedfordshire in 2006, fragments of a single Iron Age bronze mirror were recovered over an area of 300m². A lot of hoards have probably only been brought into the plough zone during the twentieth century, with the advent of deeper ploughing and more land being cultivated but some, perhaps this hoard, may have been disturbed at any time in the past fifteen hundred years and thus become widely dispersed, and possibly even substantially recovered. It is also worth mentioning that there was a gap of several years between finding the first coin and finding any further ones, despite repeated searches concentrating on the area of the find spot. In some subsequent years several turned up in a matter of days, followed by a couple of years before any more were found. Yet at no time was the plough depth increased, the cultivation methods altered, or the metal detecting equipment upgraded.

The conclusion to be drawn from this experiment is that a coin hoard that has been disturbed by agricultural cultivation is unlikely ever to be recovered in its entirety, and even after many years of metal detecting, a percentage is likely to remain. Only repeated searching with ever diminishing returns will reduce that percentage year by year.

References: Schofield, A.J. (ed.) (1991) *Interpreting Artefact Scatters*, Oxbow Books.

APPENDIX 1

Forgeries

Contemporary forgeries of coins are commonplace throughout all of the periods covered in this book, and a few examples have been included in the relevant sections. Such coins were produced to be passed off as current coin, a practice which continues to this day. In addition, since the later medieval period, replicas of coins have been produced for sale to collectors and either sold as such, or produced with the intention to deceive. Of the latter, although many are fairly crude and will rarely fool the trained eye, others are manufactured to a high standard of workmanship and require considerable skill to identify as false. Increasingly, replicas are finding their way into the ground, and if they are not identified for what they are, they may enter the record as genuine. The following are a few examples of modern replicas:

'Iron Age' die-struck gold 'quarter stater'

Cast pewter Roman 'denarius' with no markings to denote it is a replica

Roman 'denarius' with identification stamp (WRL)

Unmarked cast pewter 'Anglo-Saxon small-flan penny'

Roman 'as' with identification stamp (WRL)

Die-struck 'Anglo-Saxon broad-flan penny'

APPENDIX 2

Coin dispersal from point of issue

In 2007, a friend undertook a cycling holiday in Germany. During his stay, he took the trouble to analyse Euro coins in his change, with some interesting results. Travelling first from Trier to Koblenz and then from Heidelberg to Koblenz, 132 coins were obtained, with the countries of origin as follows:

German 105 (79.6%), Spanish 10 (7.5%), Netherlands 5 (3.7%), Luxemburg 3 (3.7%), French 2 (1.6%), Italian 2 (1.6%), Belgian 2 (1.6%), Austrian 1 (0.8%), Greek 1 (0.8%), Irish 1 (0.8%).

In the country areas the coinage was almost completely German. Luxemburg, France, Austria and Greece were encountered only in Trier and the solitary Irish coin in Heidelberg. Now given that Germany contains a network of motorways with international connections, is a centre for tourism and the country of origin of many tourists to France, Greece and Spain, it seems a remarkably immobilised result. The most likely explanation is that coins reach general circulation via banks in towns, and return to the same banks when local traders pay their takings in. Thus the majority of the coins stay local for a very long time. The general use of credit cards probably limits the amount of cash used by visitors.

This observation of coins of known volume within a known social framework allows us to make deductions, but what of other historical scenarios? Did Roman coins experience a similarly limited circulation? Many different mint marks can be seen on Roman coins in Britain, but were they imported from the mints or did they arrive in a particular locality in the pay chests of a posted legion, and like the Euros, only circulate locally? In the medieval period, when we know that there were frequent recoinages carried out from a network of regional mint towns, coin mobility as observed from single finds seems significantly greater than our Euro example, even though historically we assume the period to be one of the least mobile.

This experiment was of a small sample in a small area, and so further research is needed, but it is just one more aspect to consider when seeking to draw conclusions about coin use and loss in Britain.

APPENDIX 3

Cleaning Coins

One of the cardinal rules of coin collectors is 'never clean coins'. Collectors prize the different tones that coins acquire over the passage of time, and any harsh cleaning can drastically reduce the market value of a coin. But this book is about excavated coins, and for the most part few, except for gold, will look anything like those that appear in dealers' trays. Indeed, most ancient coins offered for sale will have been cleaned at sometime, and it is not uncommon to find bronzes that have been carefully smoothed or have had their patination enhanced in some way, although this detracts from their value.

With excavated coins that are very worn or corroded, few have any appreciable market value, and so drastic measures may be employed if only to render them legible, and in so doing give them a history that can be applied to the findspot. There are various methods, both chemical and mechanical. All are destructive, and none should be used without fully understanding the possible consequences.

Coins excavated by archaeologists are usually left to dry, and will then have earth and concretions carefully removed with wooden toothpicks and soft hair brushes. Coins recovered from ploughsoil with metal detectors are often stable enough to withstand washing and gentle brushing with a toothbrush, and sometimes even more drastic processes. Roman silver coins with a high silver content are usually robust enough to permit cleaning in dilute acid, such as a 10% solution of sulphuric acid. This will remove obscuring spots of corrosion and discoloration. Alternatively a suitable cleaning solution can be made using distilled water and citric acid crystals, which are more easily obtained than sulphuric acid. Domestic products such as lemon juice and vinegar contain impurities that could cause long-term instability in the metal and should not be used. Coins made from base silver can be prone to losing detail if placed in acid, and so it is best to treat them as copper-alloy, at least until as much has been deduced from them as is initially possible. Medieval silver coins tend to be struck in much lower relief and on thinner flans, and these respond well to electromotive reduction, a process easily effected by placing a coin in a fold of wet aluminium foil. The subsequent reaction creates heat and the emission of sulphur dioxide gas, and if the coin is then gently rubbed a contrast will be achieved between the design and background, hopefully rendering it legible and identifiable.

With copper-alloy coins, the surface metal is often entirely replaced by corrosion products, often forming a smooth glossy green patina. When subjected to corrosive chemicals, this can be stripped away, leaving an almost illegible copper core below. This is the fate of many Roman base metal coins in ploughsoil. Where a copper-alloy coin with an intact patina is recovered, the most that should be done is to gently wash the soil away with a soft bristle toothbrush, and then perhaps pick off any spots of corrosion, and finally gently brush the coin. Where a coin is more heavily encrusted, gentle chemical stripping can be used, which if carefully monitored, can help to render a coin legible. Immersion in a solution of sodium hexametaphosphate will slowly dissolve surface deposits, and will only start removing patination after some time. Complete removal of patination may render a coin completely illegible. If it is judged that a coin's surface is intact but is obscured by heavier encrustation, cleaning by electrolysis can sometimes produce a satisfactory result. Enhancement of obscured details may also be achieved by abrading the surface with a glass bristle tool, or even using a pencil eraser to highlight detail. There is no single method that can be applied to all coins, and thus it is very much a case of experience and experimentation. It must be stressed that if a coin seems to be of potential historical signifi-cance, cleaning should be left to an expert conservator, and any find that could potentially be Treasure must not be cleaned at all.

Copper token half-cleaned with glass bristle tool

APPENDIX 4

Metal Detecting

Many of the data concerning coin finds over the past thirty years have been accumulated through the use of metal detectors, and it seems appropriate to give an overview here of their development and use.

Electronic location devices have existed since the late nineteenth century, but it was only with the advent of the transistor that it became practical to build lightweight equipment capable of locating small metal objects. Metal detecting as a hobby evolved in the United States, where the units were used to search for coins and historical artefacts. Because of the relatively recent (metal using) history of the Americas, most searching was carried out in places likely to produce recent losses of coins and jewellery, and coins dating from the eighteenth or nineteenth centuries when they did occur were regarded as outstanding finds. At this stage there was little liaison between metal detector users and archaeologists, as there seemed to be little of common interest between the two groups.

When metal detectors became available in the UK, their users followed American ethics and objectives, and promotional emphasis was placed upon the quest for objects rather than knowledge. Finds were regarded as hunting trophies more than historical evidence, and considerable secrecy was engendered between rival treasure hunters who sought to keep the most productive sites to themselves. Given the historical background of Europe as opposed to America, there was an almost immediate confrontation with archaeology, which although having similar relic hunting beginnings itself, had evolved into a scientific discipline underwritten by legislation. Britain's laws pertaining to the use of metal detectors are extremely liberal when compared to most other countries; provided the operator does not venture on to land designated as a scheduled ancient monument, has the landowner's permission and follows the law on Treasure (see next chapter), there are few restrictions. Because of this, a number of attempts have been made to ban or seriously curtail the use of hobby metal detectors, and there are still those who would like to see this happen, but more pragmatic individuals on both sides have tried instead to utilise the positive aspects of the hobby. Metal detecting has produced a massive range of significant finds from locations that would never be investigated by conventional archaeological means, and this has added greatly to our knowledge of historical coin use. In consequence, following the passing of the 1996 Treasure Act, which provided greater legal protection for certain categories of find, the Portable Antiquities Scheme was set up to attempt to record as many historical finds made by the general public as possible that fell outside the remit of the Act. There is now a national network of Finds Liaison Officers (FLOs), who often work closely with metal detectorists. The fruits of this cooperation may be seen in the PAS database, which in part provided information for this book. In addition, a Code of Practice on Responsible Metal Detecting has now been agreed and endorsed by all the main detecting, heritage and landowning organisations that are involved. Full details of this may be viewed via the website of the National Council for Metal Detecting at www.ncmd.co.uk, and anyone involved with the hobby of metal detecting is urged to familiarise themselves with the Code and to adhere to it.

Despite these advances, metal detecting remains a hunting hobby, not an academic discipline, and not all detectorists choose to plot and record their finds. Many coins in poor condition are often discarded without being properly studied, resulting in rarities being overlooked, together with the loss of a significant body of statistical data. Additionally, although many hobby participants have become experts in finds identification, there is still a considerable volume of unprocessed data given to the FLOs, creating a tremendous workload for those involved in maintaining the database. Since the advent of GPS, digital imaging and simple computer software, detectorists now have the means to identify and record all their finds with relative ease, and to those detectorists who *do* record their finds the science of numismatics is greatly indebted.

APPENDIX 5

The Treasure Act

The Treasure Act came into force in September 1997, and superseded the existing law of Treasure Trove. Treasure Trove originated in the Middle Ages, and was solely intended to address the ownership of finds of buried treasure from a financial aspect, with no regard for any possible historical value. In practice this meant that if a find of treasure was made, and it could be shown that the original depositor had abandoned the treasure with no intention of recovering it, the ownership lay with the landowner. If the intention had been to recover it, the ownership lay with the Crown. In the nineteenth century it became the practice for the Crown to waive its claim in favour of any museum or institution that wished to acquire the find. Compensation to the market value of the find was then paid to the finder. This worked only in as far as the intention of the original depositor could be assessed, which with the passage of time was frequently impossible. Many finds were clearly casual losses, or votive deposits or grave goods, all of which fell outside the remit of Treasure Trove. In consequence new legislation was enacted and which is summarised as follows:

The following finds are Treasure under the Act, if found after 24 September 1997 (or, in the case of Category 2, if found after 1 January 2003)

1. Any metallic object, other than a coin, provided that at least 10% by weight of metal is gold or silver and that it is at least three hundred years old at the time of discovery. If the object is of prehistoric date it will be Treasure if any part of it contains gold or silver.

2. Any group of two or more metallic objects of any composition of prehistoric date that come from the same find (see below).

3. Any group of two or more coins that contain more than 10% of gold or silver and that are at least three hundred years old at the time of discovery.

4. Any group of ten or more coins that contain less than 10% gold and silver and that are at least three hundred years old at the time of discovery.

Only the following categories of coin find will normally be regarded as constituting a discrete group: (a) hoards that have been deliberately hidden (b) small groups such as the contents of a purse that may have been lost (c) votive or ritual deposits.

5. Any object of any material that is found in the same place or had previously been in association with another object that is Treasure.

6. Any object that would previously have been Treasure Trove, but does not fall within the specific categories above. Only objects that are less than 300 years old, that are made substantially of gold or silver, that have been deliberately hidden with the intention of recovery and whose owners or heirs are unknown will come into this category.

Note: An object or coin is part of the 'same find' as another object or coin if it is found in the same place as, or had previously been together with, the other object. Finds may have become scattered since they were originally deposited in the ground. Interpretation of this ruling requires considerable experience; coins of many periods, including gold and silver, may be found in ploughsoil but are unlikely to have ever been associated. Others however, depending on their type and context, may well have been. It is therefore in everyone's best interest to report any find that may qualify, for even if it does not, the reporting of the find still adds to our knowledge of the past. You must report all finds of Treasure to a coroner for the district in which they are found either within 14 days after the day on which you made the discovery or within 14 days after the day on which you realised the find might be treasure.

APPENDIX 6

Contacts

Finds Recording

As described in the previous chapters, only by recording new finds can researchers advance our understanding of coins and monetary use. The Portable Antiquities Scheme has a nationwide network of Finds Liaison Officers who will record coins of all earlier historic periods. Their website also contain a mine of useful information and links that will assist in understanding and identifying coin finds. The PAS website is at www.finds.org.uk. In addition, there are a number of bodies or organisations currently recording specific types of coin or token. These are the Celtic Coin Index, now under the aegis of the PAS, the Early Medieval Corpus based at the Fitzwilliam Museum in Cambridge (www.fitzmuseum.cam.ac.uk) and a project currently researching lead tokens (www.leadtokens.org.uk). All will welcome information on new finds, irrespective of rarity or condition.

Numismatic Societies

For anyone with a genuine interest in coins, they could hardly do better than to join a numismatic society, of which there are many throughout Britain. There are two national numismatic societies, both based in London, the Royal and the British. Both share a very comprehensive library of numismatic books which are available to members, and in provincial clubs there will be found many amateur experts with extensive libraries who are willing to share their knowledge.

Most numismatic societies are affiliated to the British Association of Numismatic Societies (BANS). To contact a club or society in your area, visit the BANS website at www.coinclubs.freeserve.co.uk.

Select Bibliography

There are many useful books available that can assist with identifying coins likely to be found in Britain, but the following titles are the main reference works used to catalogue such coins. In addition to those listed here there are many other titles, some long out of print, that are still cited as references in older publications.

Iron Age Coins

De la Tour, H., *Atlas de Monnaies Gauloises* (Paris, 1892, reprinted 2001).
Hobbs, R., *British Iron Age Coins in the British Museum* (London, 1996).
Van Arsdell, R., *Celtic Coinage in Britain* (London 1989).

Roman Coins

Hill, P. & Kent, J., *Late Roman Bronze Coinage* (London, 1978).
Roman Imperial Coinage (RIC) A 10 volume work written over many years, reprinted several times and subject to ongoing revision.
Sear, D., *Roman Coins and their Values* (London, 2000, 2002 and 2005. Three volumes in print, a fourth in preparation).
Sydenham, M.A., *The Coinage of the Roman Republic* (New York, 1976).

Medieval Coins

Belfort, A. de, *Description générale des monnaies mérovingiennes, vols. 1-5* (Paris 1892-5).
Boudeau, E. *Catalogue general illustré de monnaies provinciales* (Paris, reprinted 2002).
Elias, E.R.D. *The Anglo-Gallic Coins* (Paris/London, 1984).
Grierson, P. and Blackburn, M. *Medieval European Coinage, vol. 1* (Cambridge, 1986).
Mayhew, N.J. *Sterling Imitations of Edwardian Type* (London, 1983).
Metcalf, M. *Thrymsas and Sceattas, vols. 1-3* (Oxford 1993-4).
North, J.J. *English Hammered Coinage, vols. 1-2* (London 1991, 1994).
Poey d'Avant, F. *Les monnaies féodales de la France, vols. 1-3* (Paris 1858-62).
Prou, M., *Les Monnaies Carolingiannes* (Paris, 1892).
Prou, M., *Les Monnaies Mérovingiennes* (Paris, 1892).

Tokens, Jetons and Medals

Dalton, R and Hamer, S.H. *The Provincial Token-Coinage of the 18th Century (reprinted Cold Spring 1990)*
Dickinson, M., *Seventeenth Century Tokens of the British Isles* (London, 1986).
Mitchiner M., *Jetons, Medalets & Tokens, vols 1-4* (London, 1988,1991, 1998, 2008).
Seaby, *British Tokens and their Values* (London, reprinted 1984)
Williamson, G.C., *Trade Tokens issued in the Seventeenth Century, vols. 1-3* (London, reprinted 1967).

General

Coins of England and the United Kingdom. Spink Standard Catalogue of British Coins (annual publication)
Coins of Scotland, Ireland and the Islands, Pre-decimal Issues. Spink Standard Catalogue of British Coins (London 2002).
Duplessy, J., *Les Monnaies Françaises Royals, vols. 1-2* (Paris, 1988).
Krause, C.L. & Mishler, C. *Standard Catalogue of World Coins* (periodic publication)